Chopin's Poland

A guidebook to places
associated with the composer

Marita Albán Juárez
Ewa Sławińska-Dahlig

Chopin's
Poland

A guidebook to places
associated with the composer

Warsaw 2008

CONTENTS

▲ Windmill,
Pencil drawing by Fryderyk Chopin

INTRODUCTION

C hopin's Poland is an illustrated guidebook to places in Poland where Fryderyk Chopin stopped, stayed or lived. The historically inaccurate term 'Chopin's Poland' refers in some measure to the patriotic conception of the borders of Poland that was held at the time of the composer's youth. In spite of the Partitions,[1] the whole area of the Polish lands was regarded as Poland at that time. The map of Chopin's Polish journeys does not extend beyond the territory of present-day Poland. For each location, historical information is complemented with a present-day perspective.

~ The places described are grouped according to region: Mazovia, Dobrinland and Culmland, Silesia, Pomerania, Greater Poland, Lesser Poland, Chelmland.

~ Each chapter of the book contains some fixed elements: the circumstances surrounding the composer's stay, a brief history of the location (building) and a description of its current state. There is also a list of things worth seeing in each location or the surrounding area (except for the cities of Gdańsk, Kalisz, Cracow, Płock, Poznań, Toruń, Warsaw and Wrocław, where the historical buildings and sites worth visiting are so numerous that any lengthier description would disturb the proportions of the text). The most space is devoted to places associated with Chopin in Warsaw, where he lived for twenty years of his life. There are details relating to the houses, schools, concert halls and other places frequented by the composer. The identification of numerous buildings provided a basis from which to sketch the routes of daily walks, which may inspire readers to visit the city's historical sites 'in the footsteps of Chopin'.

~ The places in Polish lands where Chopin stayed are identified mainly thanks to the biographical-historical Chopin literature, but above all to mentions in the composer's correspondence. However, since not all of Chopin's letters have been preserved, and there is no wholly reliable edition of the composer's correspondence, the list is doubtless incomplete. In Warsaw alone, we certainly do not have all the exact addresses of the salons where Chopin played or the homes of the friends whom he visited.

~ The text takes account, not only of places in which Chopin lived or stayed during the summer holidays, but also of places which he merely passed through and mentioned in his correspondence. Also referred to are places in which the composer's sojourn is only hypothetical, that is, not documented by sources. The preparation of this book was accompanied by doubts that occasionally resulted from contradictory information (in the vast Chopin literature, encompassing biographies, guidebooks and albums) and from difficulties with the reconstruction of details. Many events from Chopin's life have yet to unequivocally explained.

~ Some controversy may be aroused by the lack of Cuiavia on the contents page. There are, however, no documents or mentions in Chopin's correspondence testifying that he stayed in this region. We know that in 1782, Fryderyk Chopin's mother, Tekla Justyna Krzyżanowska, entered the world on the manor farm of Długie, near Izbica Kujawska. This location is also linked to the family history of Fryderyk's grandparents, Antonina and Jakub Krzyżanowski, who spent most of their lives there.[2] In 2000, a brass plaque set in stone was unveiled in the village of Długie informing visitors that the composer's mother was born there. Unfortunately, no proof whatsoever exists of Fryderyk's contacts with his maternal or paternal grandparents. Only legends surround Chopin's visits to Cuiavia. All we know is that the composer travelled through Cuiavia (e.g. Nieszawa) while in Dobrinland in 1824: Chopin gave a colourful account of this passage in the 'Foreign News' section of his *Kuryer Szafarski* [Szafarnia courier]. From this we learn that he heard in Nieszawa a 'little mazurka' performed by a 'singer'—'some Catalani sitting on a fence'. The stanza[3] quoted by the fourteen-year-old composer is the earliest known copy of words from a song from Cuiavia[4].

~ The final section of the book contains a list of Chopin monuments, statues and commemorative plaques, as well as a bibliography, indices of names and places, and maps.

~ A crucial part of this guidebook are the reproductions of almost fifty historical illustrations and lithographs, mostly dating from the first half of the nineteenth century, as well as the most up-to-date photographic documentation of all the places described. The photographs were taken specially for the needs of this book during the period 2003–2008.

~ The state of particular sites, the cultivation of the Chopin traditions there and the care taken to preserve the composer's memory would appear to reflect human sensitivities and attitudes towards the life and work of this great Pole. Chopin himself, in a letter to Jan Białobłocki from Warsaw in 1826, requested: 'If you see Szafarnia, Płone, Gulbiny, Radomin or Ornówek, mention my name'.[5] The most important locations associated with Chopin, besides Warsaw, are Żelazowa Wola, Sanniki, Szafarnia, Duszniki Zdrój and Antonin, and today these are the main centres in Poland for the cultivation of the Chopin tradition.

~ Fryderyk Chopin's twenty-year residence in his homeland was enriched by holiday trips to the countryside—calm, quiet and picturesque, with a strongly-rooted, lively traditional culture abounding in customs and rituals of which song and music were an integral part, as we learn from Chopin's correspondence. The rural amusements, weddings and harvest festivals, the full-blooded singing, dancing 'till you drop' to the accompaniment of a band or barely 'a single fiddle – and a three-string one at that' and the rural community, which 'was engaged in whole-hearted amusement' certainly made a deep and lasting impression on the young composer. He became acquainted with the traditional music of many regions of Poland, especially Mazovia, Dobrinland and Greater Poland; he adored his stays in the country, and although they constitute barely a small percentage of the whole time he spent in Poland, they were immeasurably important in his life, his creative development and the shaping of his musical sensibilities and imagination. Their echoes can be heard throughout virtually the entire Chopin oeuvre.

~ Focussed in his homeland was that which was closest to the composer's heart and which, from the moment he entered exile, became the subject of his greatest yearning, a synonym of happiness, peace and family warmth. As he wrote in a letter from Paris in 1845: 'I'm always one foot with you'.[6]

I

Mazovia and Warsaw
(Mazowsze i Warszawa)

Żelazowa Wola

From the turn of the eighteenth and nineteenth centuries, the estate of 'Żelazowa Wola and Orły with adjoining properties' belonged to the Skarbek family. Here lived Ludwika Skarbek with her children: Fryderyk, Anastazy-Teodor, Michał, Anna and Kazimierz. Żelazowa Wola was probably the place where Chopin's parents first met: Justyna, née Krzyżanowska, helped to run the house and Mikołaj Chopin, an immigrant from France, was tutor to the children. After their wedding, the Chopins lived in the left annexe of the walled manor house, and there, on 1 March 1810, Fryderyk Chopin entered the world. His sisters, the elder Ludwika Marianna and his two younger siblings, Justyna Izabela (known as Izabela) and Emilia, were born in Warsaw. Fryderyk's childhood was not, however, associated with Żelazowa Wola, since in the autumn of 1810 the Chopin family moved to Warsaw for good. In later years, the Chopins would visit the Skarbeks at Żelazowa Wola, mainly during the summer or on religious holidays.

~ The Chopin literature contains several accounts of Fryderyk's stays in the place of his birth. He probably spent some time there in the summer of 1823. Together with his sister Ludwika he spent there also Christmas 1825 and New Year 1826. In the summer of 1830 he visited his friend Tytus Woyciechowski at Poturzyn, then stopped over for a few days in Warsaw before making his way to Żelazowa Wola, where the Chopin family was staying on a summer break. This was the composer's last stay in his birthplace.

◄ Żelazowa Wola manor

~ During his visits to the Skarbek estate, he spent a great deal of time playing music. In the summer, the piano would be taken out into the garden, where under the spruce or linden trees Fryderyk gave concerts. Besides his family and friends, these exceptional performances were heard by numerous guests, and also doubtless, by chance, the inhabitants of the nearby villages.

~ The history of Żelazowa Wola dates back to the second half of the sixteenth century, its earliest documented inhabitants and landowners being the brothers Mikołaj and Piotr Żelazo. The next identified proprietors of the estate came from the Paprocki family; it was during their times, or those of their heirs, towards the end of the eighteenth century, that the walled manor house was built. In May 1798 the Skarbeks purchased Żelazowa Wola from Piotr Łuszczewski. In 1801, after Count Kacper Skarbek had fled, leaving huge debts, the estate and all the onerous duties related to it were taken over by Countess Ludwika Skarbek. It is difficult today to judge how exactly the manor and its surroundings looked. The subject literature gives many diverging opinions on this matter. One of these (very widely held) is that part of the building was destroyed in a fire that supposedly broke out during the period of the Napoleonic Wars. This would explain how mainly the right annexe was used as living quarters. However, in light of the most recent research, this hypothesis should be rejected in favour of versions closer to descriptions contained in notarial documents. Thus it should be assumed that during the period of interest to us here, when the manor belonged to the Skarbeks, Żelazowa Wola comprised the 'Manor, Annexes, Orangery, Stables and Coach House'. The manor house itself was a typical walled building of those times and of the region, 'on a rectangular plan, with a double entrance hallway down the middle, ending with an exit onto the garden. On either side of the hallway were the rooms of the members of the household, a large dining room, a kitchen, and also a pantry, known as the treasury. It is presumed to have been covered with a "Polish" mansard-style hip-roof with a shingle thatch, as was typical of that period.'[7]

~ Żelazowa Wola was taken over[8] from Countess Ludwika Skarbek by her sons— first Fryderyk and then, in 1825, Michał, who committed suicide in 1834. The further history of the estate is not associated with the Skarbek family. Named among its successive owners are Franciszek Kwiatkowski, Józef Wiśniewski (to 1842), Henryk Peszel (to 1856) and Paweł Jaworski.[9] In the years 1859–1878[10] the manor house was inhabited by Adam Towiański, son of the famous philosopher Andrzej Towiański. It is thanks to him that the building was renovated, and also that plans were drawn up to establish a place devoted to the memory of Chopin. In 1879 the estate came into the hands of Aleksander Pawłowski, who was not interested in carrying out his predecessor's ambitious plan. As a result, the fortunes of the composer's birthplace began to be addressed by artistic milieux in Warsaw. From 1891, work began on transforming the manor house into a Chopin museum. However, the venture proved time-consuming and the formalities extremely complex, and a constant lack of funds further hampered their efforts. Assistance in the realisation of the project was given by the Warsaw Music Society, and also the composer Mily Balakirev, thanks to whom, in 1894, permission was granted to erect a commemorative obelisk on the grounds at Żelazowa Wola.

~ Not until the 1920s, when Poland regained her independence, was the building officially awarded the status of an historical building of exceptional significance

◄ Żelazowa Wola, Fryderyk Chopin's birthplace, drawing by Lenc, 1891

for Polish culture. Thanks to the efforts of the Society for the Friends of Chopin's Home, established in Warsaw, and the Chopin Committee in Sochaczew, the manor house was finally purchased, along with the park surrounding the building and several hectares of land belonging to the estate. In 1930 the Committee for the Construction of Chopin's Home initiated the manor's renovation and rebuilding, and Professor Franciszek Krzywda-Polkowski began implementing his plans for the gardens.

▲
Żelazowa Wola manor

~ Thanks to enormous help from the general public, a collection of historical items dating from the early nineteenth century was soon assembled. A Pleyel piano was brought to Żelazowa Wola, and the numerous donations also included cuttings and seedlings from around Poland and abroad, specifically intended to enrich the park with an interesting collection of dendrological specimens.

~ The outbreak of World War Two made it impossible to continue work at Żelazowa Wola. During the war, the historical piano was stolen and the manor's interiors, as well as most of the exhibits from the collection, were heavily damaged. After the war, in 1945, the Temporary Committee for the Care of Chopin's Home at Żelazowa Wola was appointed. The Committee's work was soon taken over by the Fryderyk Chopin Institute, to which, in the name of the State Treasury, the General Conservator of Historical Buildings and Artefacts entrusted the care of Żelazowa Wola.

~ Up to 1949, work continued on renovating the building, reconstructing the garden, and assembling a collection of period furniture and objects. On the centenary of Chopin's death, the display was ceremoniously opened. From 1950, Chopin's home was administered for two years by the National Museum. From

1953, the Fryderyk Chopin Society was guardian of the Żelazowa Wola estate, and on 1 August 2005 these functions were taken over by the Fryderyk Chopin Institute.

Żelazowa Wola, woodcut by I. Chełmicki, after B. Jaworski, 1870

~ In Chopin's home at Żelazowa Wola, the atmosphere of a Polish manor house from the early nineteenth century has been recreated. However, there are no objects that belonged to the composer's family. The original layout of the rooms has also been changed. Today, the house is divided by a hallway running along its centre; on its right-hand side are the hearth room, the dining room and the music room; on the left-hand side are the mother's room, the children's room and the father's study.

~ Among the items assembled in the house are a piano by Leszczyński of Warsaw, from the first half of the nineteenth century, a nineteenth-century giraffe piano by Fried, Külbors of Wrocław, nineteenth-century Biedermeier-style furniture, and portraits of Fryderyk Chopin and his family. Standing in the music room is the modern-day piano played by pianists in the Chopin concerts held during the summer season.

~ Erected in the landscape garden, rich in original plant species, which is traversed by the River Utrata, are four monuments to Fryderyk Chopin. The first of these is an obelisk resembling a gravestone, ceremoniously unveiled in 1894. This bears a

◄ Bronze statue of Fryderyk Chopin
by J. Gosławski in Żelazowa Wola

medallion with a bust of Chopin and the inscription 'F. Chopin 22. II. 1810' above a lyre ringed with leaves. This monument was designed by Bronisław Żochowski, and the composer's likeness, after a medallion by J. F. A Bovy, was produced by Jan Wojdyła.

~ Unveiled in 1968 was a sandstone bust of Chopin made by Stanisław Sikora, and the following year, on the 120th anniversary of the composer's death, a bronze statue by Józef Gosławski placed on a grey granite pedestal. The most recent work is Zofia Wolska's bronze bust of Chopin on a sandstone base, funded by the Stadtmuseum in Düsseldorf. In addition, in 1984 the Chopin Society erected near the house a rock commemorating the contribution of professor Franciszek Krzywda-Polkowski to creating the park at Żelazowa Wola.

~ Since 1954, a season of Chopin concerts has been held annually, from the first Sunday in May to the last Sunday in September. These recitals were initiated by the pianist and pedagogue Zbigniew Drzewiecki. A separate initiative, from 2006, is the programme of Music Presentations showcasing young pianists held during the same period (May–September).

The village of Żelazowa Wola is situated in Sochaczew county, on the edge of Kampinos Forest, 54 km from Warsaw. It is the most famous 'shrine' to the composer in Poland, visited in great number by tourists and music lovers from Poland and abroad.

Worth seeing in the area:
▶ Trojanów church, in late Baroque style, reconstructed after a fire in the first quarter of the twentieth century.
▶ Chodaków cemetery, for soldiers killed in the Battle of Bzura.

Brochów

THE PARISH CHURCH OF ST ROCH (now St John the Baptist) in Brochów was a particularly important place in the family history of both the Skarbeks and the Chopins. Here, on 2 June 1806, the wedding was held of the composer's parents, Mikołaj Chopin and Tekla Justyna Krzyżanowska. In this same church, on Easter Sunday, 23 April 1810, Fryderyk Franciszek Chopin was baptised. Although the Chopins regarded Fryderyk Skarbek as their son's godfather, it is Franciszek Grembecki, of Ciepliny, who is entered in the certificate of baptism, possibly as proxy during the ceremony. The godmother was Anna Skarbek, later Wiesiołowska. Fryderyk was also given an 'emergency baptism', which may have taken place shortly after his birth at Żelazowa Wola, in the presence of Countess Ludwika Skarbek.[11]

~ Besides the entries of the Chopins' wedding and little Fryderyk's baptism, the Brochów church records also carried an entry relating to the wedding of the composer's sister, Ludwika, who in 1832 married in her family parish Józef Kalasanty Jędrzejewicz. It is highly likely that the members of the Chopin family combined every stay at Żelazowa Wola with visits to Brochów.

~ The first church in Brochów was probably built before 1113, during the reign of Ladislaus Herman. Over two hundred years later, in 1351, work began on the construction of a brick church, and a further two centuries later, in the years 1551–61, its rebuilding. Conservation work, completed in 1665, was last carried out by Olbracht Adrian Lasocki, husband of Agnieszka Brochowska.

~ Situated on the banks of the Bzura, this Renaissance-style building of fortified character is an exceptional example of Polish sacred architecture. Built of red brick, the church is crowned with three towers. Two of these stand either side of the Romanesque portal, the third above the presbytery. The grounds are enclosed by a wall with corner bastions.

~ In 1993 a commemorative plaque was installed inside Brochów church, on the left-hand side of the nave. Its inscription reads as follows: 'Baptised in this church on 23 April 1810 was Fryderyk Chopin, born on 22 February 1810 at Żelazowa Wola'. The history of the parish, as recorded on another plaque on one of the church's pillars, mentions Brochów's connections with the Chopin family.

~ Not far from the church, on the manor grounds, a Masterclass Centre is currently being built, where outstanding young pianists from all over the world will be able to hone their skills under the guidance of outstanding Chopin interpreters. Since 2006, Chopin recitals have been held in the church every Sunday during July and August.

Church of St John
the Baptist in Brochów

~ A sculpture of the first patron, St Roch, standing near the church, is surrounded by slender birches. Flat fields extend all around, with rows of old willows.

▲ Church of St Roch in Brochów, drawing signed 'Wł. Gościmski'

Brochów is situated 11 km north of Żelazowa Wola.

Worth seeing in the area:
► Classicist manor house with coach house, in an historical landscape garden, at Tułowice.
► Next to the bridge over the Bzura at Witkowice, a plaque and monument commemorating the Polish troops' crossing of the river during the Battle of Bzura (1939).

Warsaw: Saxon Palace (Pałac Saski)

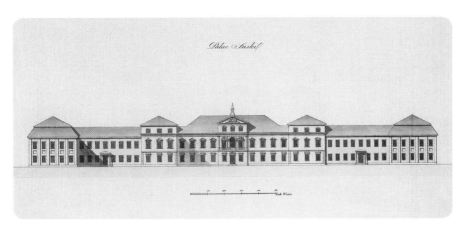

I N SEPTEMBER 1810 the Chopin family moved for good to Warsaw. Samuel Bogumił Linde offered Fryderyk's father the post of French teacher to the lower years at the Warsaw Lyceum secondary school. The Chopins moved into a second floor apartment in the right wing of the Saxon Palace (ul. Krakowskie Przedmieście, plot no. 413). This building housed the Lyceum and the flats of its teachers.

~ In 1817 Grand Duke Constantine had the palace appropriated for military purposes, and the school and its teachers were moved to Casimir Palace.

~ At the beginning of the eighteenth century, Augustus II the Strong purchased several mansions belonging to the Lubomirski, Sapieha and Morsztyn families and then had them rebuilt and joined together, giving rise to the splendid edifice known as the Saxon Palace. After 1797, the building became government property. During rebuilding work carried out in the first half of the nineteenth century a grand colonnade was added in the middle section.

~ The arcade on Plac Piłsudskiego surrounding the Tomb of the Unknown Soldier is the only part of the Saxon Palace to have escaped destruction during World War Two.

~ The Tomb of the Unknown Soldier [Grób Nieznanego Żołnierza] by the colonnade of the Saxon Palace has been in place since 1925. Initially, it was devoted to the memory of Poles who had perished in combat during the periods 1914–18 and 1918–20. In 1925 the body of an unknown soldier removed from the Cemetery of the Defenders of Lviv was ceremoniously laid to rest in the Tomb.

▲ Saxon Palace, colour lithograph by L. Schmidtner, first half of 19th c.

(21)

▲ Arcade of the Tomb
of the Unknown Soldier
[Grób Nieznanego Żołnierza]

~ The architectural conception and design of the Tomb of the Unknown Solder were the work of Stanisław Ostrowski. During World War Two, the Saxon Palace and the Tomb were destroyed. Since 1946, the mutilated palace arcade has served as the backdrop to the restored tomb. Lain inside the tomb are urns containing the ashes of fallen soldiers and earth from battlefields. Placed on a marble slab is an eternal flame and on the walls of the columns surrounding the tomb—eighteen plaques commemorating the sites of battles and the martyrdom of Poles, from the Battle of Cedynia[12] to World War Two. The spaces between the columns on the side of the Saxon Garden are filled with grills bearing representations of the three highest Polish military awards: the Virtuti Militari Military Order, the Cross of the Brave and the Grunwald Cross. The decoration, grills and torches were designed by Henryk Grunwald. Every Sunday a ceremonial changing of the guard is held by the tomb, paying tribute to Poles killed in battle. This site is frequently visited by foreign government delegations staying in the capital.

Warsaw: Saxon Garden (Ogród Saski)

FRYDERYK CHOPIN SPENT HIS FIRST SEVEN YEARS OF LIFE in the Saxon Palace, and so in the direct vicinity of the Saxon Garden. Mrs Justyna Chopin will certainly have taken Ludwika and little Frycek to the nearby park. Given Fryderyk's fondness for walks around the city, we can assume that a dozen years or so later he visited this beautiful spot on many occasions in the company of friends. Some biographers have even held that he used to come here with Konstancja Gładkowska, although there is no information regarding such romantic walks in mentions of Fryderyk's contacts with his first love.

~ The Saxon Garden was part of the 'Saxon Axis'—a complex of royal residences and gardens belonging to Augustus II the Strong, created in the years 1713–33 to the king's commission by Jan Krzysztof Naumann and Mateusz Daniel Pöppelmann. By 1727 the Garden had become the first public park in Warsaw. During Chopin's lifetime, it was redesigned by James Savage in the spirit of an English landscape garden.

~ Today the Saxon Garden adjoins Plac Piłsudskiego and also ul. Marszałkowska and ul. Królewska. On the Plac Piłsudskiego side, one is drawn to a magnificent chalice-shaped fountain from 1855, designed by Henryk Marconi, who also designed the classicist water tower, known as the

▲ Saxon Garden

Poranek w Ogrodzie Instytutu sztucznych Wod mineralnych czyli Nowy Karlsbad w Warszawie.

'reservoir' [*wodozbiór*], erected on a man-made hill in 1854, surrounded by gingkos brought from Japan and China in the eighteenth century. Also striking are the late baroque sandstone sculptures, renovated in the years 1994–98. Standing by the garden's central avenue is a sundial, founded in the nineteenth century by Antoni Magier (1762–1837), a meteorologist, physicist and diarist. In the second half of the twentieth century two new monuments appeared in the park: to Stefan Starzyński (by Ludwika Kraskowska-Nitschowa) and Maria Konopnicka (by Stanisław Kulon).

▲ Saxon Garden, Mineral Water Pavilion, lithograph by F. Bruder

Warsaw: Casimir Palace (Pałac Kazimierzowski)

O N THEIR REMOVAL from the Saxon Palace in March 1817, the Chopin family spent the next ten years in a spacious apartment on the second floor of the left annexe of Casimir Palace on ul. Krakowskie Przedmieście. There the Chopins ran a renowned boarding home for boys, mainly from outside Warsaw, who either learned on site or else attended the Warsaw Lyceum (in the main building of Casimir Palace). From passages in the memoirs of ex-boarders, we can surmise that in the Chopins' modest, but exceptionally well-kept, home there reigned a friendly atmosphere and, in spite of the daily practice in French, Polish customs prevailed. Other teachers and their families lived in the near vicinity, e.g. Samuel Bogumił Linde and Juliusz Henryk Kolberg.

~ The construction of the palace was completed in 1634. It originally belonged to the wife of King John II Casimir, Maria Ludwika [Marie-Louise] Gonzaga, and served as the royal summer residence. Successive owners were John III Sobieski, his son Konstanty, Augustus II the Strong and Augustus III. In the years 1765–95 the building was home to the Knights' School, founded by King Stanislaus Augustus. From 1815 it housed the Warsaw Lyceum and the Royal University of Warsaw, and newly established academic institutions also had their seats there.

▲ Left annexe
of Casimir Palace

~ The left annexe of Casimir Palace, which the Chopins inhabited, belongs to Warsaw University. It houses, among others, the Institute of Oriental Studies and the Institute of the History of Art.

▲ Casimir Palace, water colour by J. F. Piwarski, *c.*1824 (left annexe to the right)

~ Set into the gable wall of the palace's left annexe, at first-floor level, are a bas-relief featuring a likeness of Chopin after a medallion by J. F. A. Bovy and a plaque commemorating the composer's residence, with the following inscription: 'In this building lived Fryderyk Chopin in the years 1817–1827'.

Warsaw: 'Botanika'

park behind Casimir Palace

I N CHOPIN'S DAY, part of this land was given over to a small botanical garden. Fryderyk wrote in a letter to Jan Białobłocki that the Chopins possessed
a key to the garden, which was his favourite place for playing near his home.
In later years, as a pupil of the Warsaw Lyceum, he would often walk around 'Botanika' or read there.

~ The present-day Casimir Park is situated, as in the nineteenth century, beneath
the complex of buildings of Warsaw University, at the back of Casimir Palace. On
the opposite side, a complex of greenery borders with ul. Browarna. In recent years
the land has been spruced up, and it is once again a fine place for a stroll; the park
is adorned by trees, lawns and colourful flower beds.

▲ Casimir Park ('Botanika')

Warsaw: Czapski/Krasiński Palace [Pałac Czapskich/Krasińskich]

I N 1827, FOLLOWING THE DEATH OF EMILKA, Fryderyk's youngest sister, the Chopins moved to a larger apartment, rented in the left wing of Krasiński Palace on ul. Krakowskie Przedmieście (plot no. 410). Here Fryderyk was given his own room to work in. In a letter to Tytus Woyciechowski of 27 December 1828 he wrote: 'Upstairs there is already a room that is to serve my comfort [...] There I am to have an old piano and an old bureau; it is to be my own place of refuge'.[13]
~ In his room 'in the garret' upstairs, Fryderyk was often visited by his friends on their way to the university. The Chopins' apartment was a very special place, visited by numerous artists, scholars and young men, including Samuel Bogumił Linde, Kajetan Koźmian, Juliusz Kolberg, Antoni Brodowski, Józef Elsner, Stefan Witwicki and Bohdan Zaleski. Rehearsals with orchestra musicians were also held there. At the beginning of 1830, at special musical soirees organised at the Chopins' home, a group of the composer's friends, musicians and columnists listened to the premiere performances of both piano concertos.

◄ Left wing of Czapski/ Krasiński Palace

▼ View of ul. Krakowskie Przedmieście with Czapski/ Krasiński Palace on the right-hand side, aquatint by K. F. Dietrich, 1830

1832 Salon Chopinów w Pałacu krasińskich - Rysunek at kolegom dnia 2 petrii ó illieg - po wyjeździe Fryderyka - Oryginał posiadam numla 4 ryse -

~ The Palace of Wincenty Krasiński housed the last apartment in Warsaw inhabited by Fryderyk Chopin (until 2 November 1830).

▲ The Chopins' drawing-room in Czapski/Krasiński Palace, quill sketch by A. Kolberg, 1832

~ Czapski/Krasiński Palace (earlier known as Sieniawski/Raczyński Palace) is located at 5 ul. Krakowskie Przedmieście, opposite the gate to Warsaw University. The building has been rebuilt many times and has belonged successively to the Radziwiłł, Radziejowski, Prażmowski, Sieniawski, Czartoryski and, finally, Czapski families. Thanks to rebuilding work initiated by Stanisław Małachowski and his wife Konstancja, née Czapska, in the mid eighteenth century the palace gained a late baroque character. Added around the turn of the eighteenth and nineteenth centuries were two classicist annexes, designed by J. C. Kamzetzer. In the first half of the nineteenth century the building was acquired by Wincenty Krasiński (it was inherited from the Czapskis by Krasiński's wife, Maria Urszula Radziwiłł, Countess of Nieśwież). As already mentioned, an apartment in the left wing of the palace was rented from 1827 by the Chopins. This building also housed the school attended by the poet Cyprian Kamil Norwid. In the middle of the century the library collection of the Krasiński entail estate was installed in the corner annexes. Further rebuilding brought wholesale changes to the palace's exterior, as well as its decorations and furnishings.

▲ Czapski/Krasiński Palace

∼ During the period from 1909 to the outbreak of World War Two the building belonged to Edward Raczyński, President of the Republic of Poland in Exile during the years 1979–1986. In its post-war reconstruction, it regained its appearance from the eighteenth century. Since the 1950s the palace has been the seat of the Academy of Fine Arts.

∼ In 1930 a commemorative plaque was set into the front wall of the left wing of Czapski/Krasiński Palace, on the ul. Krakowskie Przedmieście side. Its inscription reads as follows: 'In this house Fryderyk Chopin lived and worked before leaving Warsaw for good in 1830'.

∼ In the left wing, a small museum was created in the place where the Chopins apartment once stood; known as the Chopin Family Drawing Room, it was opened to the public in 1960. The interior and decor of a drawing-room from the first half of the nineteenth century were reconstructed from sketches made by Antoni Kolberg in 1832.

∼ The salon does not contain any items once belonging to the Chopin family. Besides the nineteenth-century furniture, there is a grand piano from the first half of the nineteenth century, a Pleyel upright from the same period, and also portraits of Chopin's sisters, his mother, Wojciech Żywny and Józef Elsner, as well as views of nineteenth-century Warsaw.

Warsaw: Warsaw Lyceum
[Liceum Warszawskie]

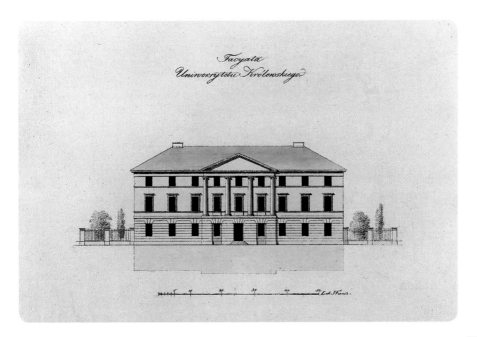

F RYDERYK BEGAN his secondary schooling in 1823, entering at the fourth
year, having previously been taught at home. He learned without difficulty
and completed his classes with distinction. During his three years at the
Warsaw Lyceum, housed in the main building of Casimir Palace, he was friendly
with Dominik Dziewanowski, Jan Matuszyński, Wilhelm Kolberg, Julian Fontana,
Marceli Celiński and Konstanty Pruszak, and also became much closer with Tytus
Woyciechowski, whom he had met earlier.

▲ Casimir Palace, lithograph
by L. Schmidtner,
second half of 19th c.

◄ Casimir Palace

Warsaw: Conservatory [Konserwatorium]

W ARSAW CONSERVATORY was housed in a building (now non-existent) that had formerly been part of a Cistercian monastery, on the corner of ul. Krakowskie Przedmieście and what was then ul. Mariensztat. It existed from 1819, but its formal inauguration as the Institute of Music and Declamation only took place in April 1821. Held here were mainly lessons for vocal and instrumental classes, as well as all practical lessons for students of the High School of Music. School concerts were held in the Conservatory's concert hall, with Fryderyk often among the performers. At one of these concerts, he met a pupil from the vocal class, Konstancja Gładkowska—the great love of his youth.

~ On the first floor of the 'ex-Cistercian' school building, on the ul. Mariensztat side, the vice-chancellor Józef Elsner had his apartment. Chopin was the vice-chancellor's favourite pupil, and so was a frequent guest in his home, where he would present his latest compositions in front of Mrs Elsner and the couple's daughter, Emilia. The same building was also home to a boarding house for female pupils of the Conservatory. There lived Konstancja Gładkowska, on whom Fryderyk frequently called. During his visits he would improvise on the piano and accompany her as she sang. The young singer's teacher, Carlo Soliva, a great admirer of Chopin's talent, was enthusiastic about these meetings. After all, he could not have dreamt of a better accompanist for his pupil.

~ A building housing a monastery was in existence on ul. Krakowskie Przedmieście, between the Royal Castle [Zamek Królewski] and the Church of St Anne, as early as the end of the fifteenth century. From 1584 it was occupied by Bernardine Franciscan Sisters. In the seventeenth century a jurisdiction was established here; the Church of St Clare was erected and a new monastic house was built. The Bernardine Sisters took care of orphans and widows, and also ran a school for girls from noble houses. In 1818 the convent was transferred to Przasnysz, and the abandoned building was converted into military stores. It was subsequently allocated to the Music Conservatory, which had its seat there until 1831.
~ The building was demolished in the 1840s, and since that time no other edifice has been erected in its place. An empty square has remained, which today offers a panoramic view over the Praga district of Warsaw.

◄ The monastery buildings on the left
housed the Music Conservatory.
B. Belotto [Canaletto],
aquatint after his own oil painting, 1771.

Warsaw: Royal University of Warsaw [Królewski Uniwersytet Warszawski]

I N THE YEARS 1826–29 Chopin attended the High School of Music [Główna Szkoła Muzyki], which constituted a Music Department, or part of the Department of Fine Arts, of Warsaw University. Although theoretical lessons were held in the university classrooms and lecture halls, the university authorities wished practical lessons in playing and composition to take place outside the school grounds, in the building of the Conservatory, in the vicinity of the Royal Castle.

~ Attendance at the High School of Music entitled pupils to attend university lectures. However, every student had to gain approval for his plans, from both Vice-Chancellor Elsner and Dean Bentkowski. In the autumn of 1826 Fryderyk wrote to Jan Białobłocki: 'I have counterpoint with Elsner precisely 6 hours a week; I attend the lectures of Brodziński, Bentkowski and of other subjects that have some kind of link with music.'[14]

~ It is not certain that Fryderyk attended the lectures referred to in the letter cited above in a systematic way, since analysis of the university timetables reveals that they clashed with obligatory lessons with Elsner, which were the most important for the young musician. We do know, however, that Chopin certainly took part in singing lessons given by Walenty Kratzer.

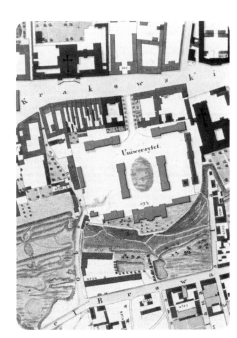

◄ Plac Zamkowy
   [Castle Square]

▶ Map of Warsaw University campus
   and 'Botanika', 1817–18

Dom Król. Towarzystwa Przyaciół Nauk

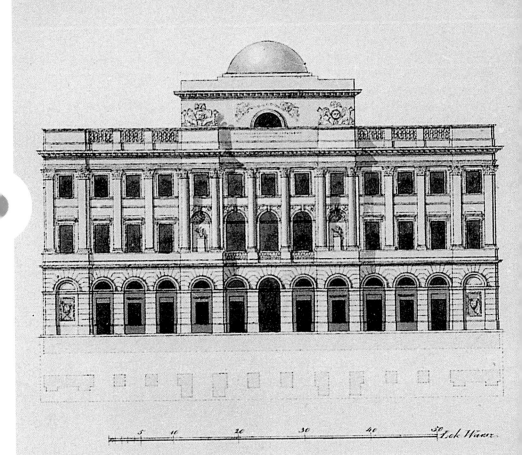

5   10   20   30   40   50 Łok Warsz.

J. Schmutner

Warsaw: Library [Biblioteka]

I N THE UNIVERSITY LIBRARY, then located in the main building of Casimir
Palace, Chopin studied music scores, as well as literature and periodicals de-
voted to music. An equally valuable collection for him was the library of the
Warsaw Society for the Friends of Learning, located in the building now known as
Staszic Palace on ul. Nowy Świat.

~ Staszic Palace [Pałac Staszica] was built in the years 1820–23 to a design by Antonio Corazzi, on the site of the eighteenth-century church of the Dominican Observers. During the last decade of the nineteenth century, the ruling Russian par-
titioners had the palace rebuilt as an Orthodox church in Ruthenian Byzantine
style. In the years 1924–26 Marian Lalewicz returned the building to its classicist
character. Post-war reconstruction to a design by Piotr Biegański restored the archi-
tectonic form given the building by Corazzi. Today, the palace is the seat of the
Polish Academy of Sciences [Polska Akademia Nauk] and the Warsaw Society of
Learning [Towarzystwo Naukowe Warszawskie].

▲ Staszic Palace [Pałac Staszica]

◄ Home of the Warsaw Society for the Friends
of Learning, lithograph by L. Schmidtner,
first half of 19th c.

~ In front of the palace stands a monument to Copernicus by Bertel Thorvaldsen, erected and ceremoniously unveiled in 1830. During the war the monument was partly destroyed and then transported by the Germans to the West. In 1945 it returned to its former location, and four years later regained its original appearance.

~ Both the building and the monument were erected at the initiative and through the efforts of the then chair of the Society for the Friends of Learning, the eminent writer, philosopher and scholar, Stanisław Staszic (1755–1826). On his death, his body was laid out in the palace and subsequently laid to rest by the Camaldolese church of the Immaculate Conception of the Blessed Virgin Mary in the Bielany district of the city. Present at the funeral was Chopin, who included an extensive account of the ceremony in a letter to Jan Białobłocki. Staszic's grave and bust are situated by the left-hand wall of the church (looking from the main entrance). The Camaldolese church was erected in the years 1669–1710. It stands on ul. Dewajtis, in Bielany Forest, not far from Cardinal Stefan Wyszyński University.

Warsaw: Learning foreign languages

D URING HIS STUDIES, Chopin, together with Tytus Woyciechowski and Karol Weltz, attended Italian lessons, given by 'a certain Rinaldi', and also private English lessons, which Wilhelm Kolberg described in his memoirs: 'In 1829 I was living on ul. Krakowskie Przedmieście in a tenement house on the corner of ul. Oboźna; Chopin and his parents lived in Krasiński Palace. He came to me three evenings a week for English lessons, which we took with Julian Fontana from a teacher of Irish extraction well known in Warsaw at that time, Makartnej [sic] [...] These lessons were enlivened by an extraordinary contest of concepts, gestures and jests, initiated for the most part by Chopin.'[15]

Warsaw: Radziwiłł Palace
[Pałac Radziwiłłowski]

ADZIWIŁŁ PALACE, now also known as the Presidential Palace [Pałac Prezydencki], situated on ul. Krakowskie Przedmieście (two hundred years ago at no. 387) is believed to have been the venue for Fryderyk Chopin's first public performance. The concert took place on 24 February 1818 and was organised at the initiative of Countess Zofia Zamoyska by the Warsaw Charitable Society, chaired at that time by Julian Ursyn Niemcewicz. The brilliant young pianist, then eight years old, performed a piano concerto by Gyrowetz.[16]

~ Radziwiłł Palace was built in the seventeenth century. It belonged in turn to the Koniecpolski and Lubomirski families, but was owned for the longest period by the Radziwiłłs. At the beginning of the eighteenth century it was rebuilt in classicist style, and in 1821 stone lions, designed by Camillo Landini, were placed on the street side of the palace. In 1817 the palace was purchased from the Radziwiłłs and became the seat of the Tsarist Governor. After the First World War, the building housed the Presidium of the Council of Ministers; since 1994 it has been the seat of the President of the Polish Republic and the venue for meetings and talks with official guests of the head of state.

▲ Radziwiłł Palace

▲ Radziwiłł Palace, lithograph by K. F. Dietrich, first half of 19th c.

∼ The largest and most splendid interiors in the palace are the Column Hall and the White Room.

Situated on the second floor are the private rooms of the President and his family. The side wings house the press office, the spokesman's office, the President's Office and other official rooms. The entrance to the courtyard is still guarded by four stone lions and an equestrian monument of Prince Józef Poniatowski by Bertel Thorvaldsen from the end of the 1820s. This was initially placed in front of the Saxon Palace, and then by the Old Orangery in the Royal Baths Park. It was moved to its present location in 1965. At the back of the palace extends a garden in which banquets and other ceremonies are held.

◄ Radziwiłł Palace

Warsaw: Warsaw Charitable Society [Warszawskie Towarzystwo Dobroczynności]

O N 24 FEBRUARY 1823 the Warsaw Charitable Society organised another concert in which Chopin performed. This time it was held at the Society's headquarters (the building 'Res Sacra Miser'), a classicistic building on ul. Krakowskie Przedmieście (corner with ul. Bednarska), erected in the years 1818–19 by Antonio Corazzi.

~ Following its wartime destruction, the 'Res Sacra Miser' building was reconstructed to its original design; today it is the seat of Caritas, a Catholic association for relief, development and social service. It also houses the Roman Catholic Rector's Chapel of the Immaculate Conception of the Blessed Virgin Mary and the Resursa academic bookshop.

▲ Building of the Warsaw Charitable Society, lithograph by K. Pilatti

◄ 'Res Sacra Miser' building

Warsaw: Belvedere [Belweder]

AFTER THE YEAR 1822, the young Fryderyk, who had already gained a reputation as a talented pianist, was a regular guest of Grand Duke Constantine and his wife, Joanna, née Grudzińska. During his visits in the picturesquely situated Belvedere he not only gave concerts, but also spent time playing in the Royal Baths Park.

~ The Belvedere adjoins the Royal Baths Park. It was built in the seventeenth century, but only gained its classicist character following its rebuilding at the beginning of the nineteenth century, carried out by Jakub Kubicki. From 1818 it was the residence of Grand Duke Constantine.

~ The building only came into the possession of the Polish state when Poland regained her independence. It was the residence of Marshal Józef Piłsudski, as was commemorated several years ago with a splendid monument made by Jan Konarski, situated immediately next to the palace. After the Marshal's death, in the years 1935–39 the Belvedere was home to the Piłsudski Museum. The building luckily escaped destruction during World War Two, as it was one of the residences of the occupying German authorities.

~ In February 1848 the Fryderyk Chopin Institute organised at the Belvedere, in the Pompeian Room, a concert by Raoul Koczalski (a pupil of one of Chopin's own pupils), transmitted by Polish Radio. The pianist performed Chopin repertory on a piano that once belonged to the composer.

~ The palace, situated on the boundary with the Royal Baths Park in Warsaw, is located at 54/56 ul. Belwederska and today is one of the residences of the President of the Republic of Poland. It retains a classicist character, gained during the years 1818–22, when it was thoroughly rebuilt to a design by Jakub Kubicki. Among the most impressive interiors is the Pompeian Room.

◄ Belvedere Palace

▶ Belvedere, lithograph
by K. F. Dietrich,
first half of 19th c.

Warsaw: Royal Baths Park [Łazienki Królewskie]

IN 1766 KING STANISLAUS AUGUSTUS purchased the Royal Baths Park as a royal summer residence. In Chopin's day, in 1817, the complex became the property of Tsar Alexander I. Up to the 1820s, the park, adjoining the Belvedere palace and grounds, was closed to the inhabitants of Warsaw. Favoured because of his talent, the young Fryderyk was able to play here with Pawełek[17] and Moriolka[18].

~ The Royal Baths Park is a palace-garden complex situated in the Ujazdów district of Warsaw, occupying an area of almost eighty hectares. The park's name derives from the baroque bathing pavilion known as the Łazienki. This was the first building on this site, erected in the second half of the seventeenth century. Situated on an island surrounded by canals, the richly decorated pavilion was built by Tylman van Gameren for the Grand Crown Marshal Stanisław Herakliusz Lubomirski, the owner of Ujazdów.

~ In the second half of the eighteenth century the estate became the property of King Stanislaus Augustus. The entire complex of buildings dates from this period, including the Old Orangery [Stara Pomarańczarnia], the White House [Biały Domek], the amphitheatre on the island and the Myślewicki Palace [Pałac Myślewicki]. In 1772 work began on converting the bathing pavilion into the king's summer residence. This involved wholesale changes to the building's exterior, which ultimately gained a classicist character. In the interiors, however, part of the former baroque decor was retained. Henceforth the building was known as the Palace on the Water or the Palace on the Island [Pałac na Wodzie/Wyspie]. All the buildings on the grounds of the Royal Baths Park were surrounded by broad avenues for walking, with the whole park complemented by stylishly designed gardens.

~ In the nineteenth century several new classicist-style buildings were erected in the park, and further changes were also made to its spatial organisation.

~ During World War Two only a miracle prevented the buildings from being blown up. In spite of war-time destruction, it was possible to completely restore the historical buildings of the Royal Baths Park and create a museum-garden complex open to the general public.

~ The Chopin Monument in the Royal Baths Park, the work of Wacław Szymanowski, although initially controversial, is among the most beautiful and best known in Poland. Unveiled in 1926, it stands on a pool, near the main gate to the park, on Al. Ujazdowskie. In 1940 it was one of the first monuments to be destroyed by the Nazis. Hence the inscription that

◄ Palace on the Water
in the Royal Baths Park

adorns the base today: 'Statue of Fryderyk Chopin, destroyed and plundered by the Germans on 31 May 1940, rebuilt by the Nation. 17 October 1946'.

⁓ After the war, in 1958 the monument was faithfully reconstructed and replaced on its original spot. The surrounding area was designed by Oskar Sosnowski. Also engraved on the base are these words by Adam Mickiewicz:

Płomień rozgryzie malowane dzieje,
Skarby mieczowi spustoszą złodzieje,
Pieśń ujdzie cało...
[Flames will consume our painted history,
Sword-wielding thieves will plunder our treasures,
The song will be saved...]

⁓ Since 1959, Chopin concerts have been held by the monument on Sundays from the beginning of May to the end of September.

▲ View of the Palace on the Water
in the Royal Baths Park,
J. V. Fleck, first half of 19th c.

◄ Chopin Monument
by Wacław Szymanowski
in the Royal Baths Park

Warsaw: Morsztyn Palace
[Pałac Morsztynów]

O N 19 DECEMBER 1829 Chopin gave a concert in the old seat of the Merchants' Club in Morsztyn Palace, at what is now 10 ul. Miodowa. An account of this performance appeared in the press the following day: 'The members of the Merchants' Club [...] spent yesterday's musical soiree at the Club most pleasantly. It began with a concerto played by Mr Bielawski with orchestral accompaniment; he was followed by Mr Copello singing to the accompaniment of Mr Chopin. The singing of Mr Dorville, an artist of the French theatre, was accompanied by Mr Soliva, then the listeners were entertained by Mr Bielawski, playing solo, and fantasies by Mr Chopin with various well-known melodies rounded off the evening.'[19]

~ The building dates back to the end of the seventeenth century, since when it has been rebuilt many times. The first to make alterations was Stanisław Morsztyn, followed by Bishop

◄ Morsztyn Palace

Młodziejowski. Situated here for some time towards the end of the eighteenth century was the Russian embassy, which became the object of attacks by insurrectionaries in 1794. Considerably damaged, it was rebuilt in classicist style at the beginning of the nineteenth century. In the 1820s it was the property of the Association of Warsaw Merchants. In 1829 there was a schism in the association and the so-called Merchants' Club transferred its headquarters to ul. Krakowskie Przedmieście.

~ Today Morsztyn Palace is the seat of the PWN academic publishing house.

Wacu Ordynata *yskiego obok Ko"* Reformatów.

Vue du Palais de l'*
Comte Zamoyski du
Du Couvent de

Warsaw: Blue Palace [Pałac Błękitny]

T HE SALON OF COUNT Stanisław Kostka Zamoyski and Zofia Zamoyska in the Blue Palace, active from the times of the Grand Duchy of Warsaw, was one of the more important meeting points for Warsaw society. It attracted representatives of political spheres, the Russian imperial authorities (dignitaries of the Russian court and foreign guests), literary circles (especially during the period of the famous 'literary Fridays') and also musicians (organisers and performers of concerts in aid of the Charitable Society founded by the countess).

~ Chopin, who is believed to have first played at the Zamoyski salon as a sixteen-year-old, was invited to the Blue Palace many times as a young man. One of these recitals took place in May 1826. Chopin recalled that evening in a letter to Jan Białobłocki: 'On Sunday, a week ago to the day, I was at the Zamoyskis', where Długosz's aeolopantalon was admired virtually the whole evening long.'[20]

~ It is worth mentioning that in the same palace, on the ul. Żabia side, Chopin's friend, the writer Klementyna Tańska, later Hoffmanowa, also held a salon in which the young Fryderyk performed.

~ The Blue Palace was erected in the seventeenth century, and in the following century King Augustus II had it rebuilt according to a rococo design by Joachim Daniel Jauch. Subsequent owners were the Czartoryskis and, from 1811, the Zamoyskis. The next rebuilding, carried out by Fryderyk A. Lessel in late classicist style, gave the building its ultimate form, which can be admired today thanks to its post-war reconstruction.

~ On the other side of ul. Senatorska, virtually opposite the Blue Palace, stands a late baroque statue of St John Nepomucen by Giovanni Liverotti from 1731. This is one of the few original elements characteristic of this site. Located near Plac Bankowy, in the direction of Plac Teatralny, at 37 ul. Senatorska, it now houses the offices of the Municipal Transport Board, among others.

◄ The Blue Palace,
fragment of a lithograph
by K. F. Dietrich,
first half of 19th c.

▶ The Blue Palace

Warsaw: National Theatre [Teatr Narodowy]

THE THEATRE BUILDING, designed by Bonawentura Solari, was erected in 1779 on Plac Krasińskich, opposite Krasiński Palace, also known as the Palace of the Republic. It was built at the initiative of King Stanislaus Augustus, who entrusted the organising of the theatre and all rights connected with the work of the troupe to Franciszek Ryx, his trusted valet. The first performance was held on 7 September that year. The theatre was the largest and most important in Poland, and functioned until 1833, when it was transferred to a new building in the Marywil part of the city, on what is now Plac Teatralny. The old theatre building on Plac Krasińskich was converted into a warehouse and in 1874 demolished.

◄ Plac Krasińskich, with the building of the National Theatre on the right, fragment of a coloured steel engraving by Nasi, after a drawing by K. F. Dietrich, first half of 19th c.

▼ Site of the old National Theatre, now occupied by the Warsaw Rising Monument and the Supreme Court, opposite Krasiński Palace

~ Among the most outstanding creative artists to have contributed to the development of the National Theatre in this period were Wojciech Bogusławski, Józef Elsner and Karol Kurpiński. All three men attached great importance to the standard and variety of theatre presentations, created a large part of the Polish operatic repertory and also had a decisive influence on recruiting for the theatre the best actors and musicians in Warsaw.

~ Doubtless none of the artistic events of the 1820s escaped the attention of the young Chopin, who had the opportunity of admiring

▲ Building of the National Theatre, first half of 19th c.

the artistry of many Polish and foreign virtuosos, such as Maria Szymanowska, Johann Nepomuk Hummel, Stephen Heller, Niccolò Paganini, Karol Lipiński and Henriette Sontag. His friends and colleagues from the Conservatory also appeared on the boards of the national stage, including Ignacy Feliks Dobrzyński. The theatre was a place in which he regularly met with Konstancja Gładkowska at shows and rehearsals. Chopin's first grand public concert in Warsaw took place in the National Theatre on 17 March 1830: 'The universal wish of music lovers is to be granted: Mr Szopę (Chopin), so rightfully adored, whose talent is compared by connoisseurs with the foremost virtuosos, is shortly to give a piano concert at the National Theatre, performing works of his own composition.'[21]

~ The repertory did indeed comprise works by Chopin himself, including the Concerto in F minor, Op. 21 and *Fantasy on Polish Airs*, Op. 13, performed with the accompaniment of an orchestra directed by Karol Kurpiński. A second performance, with a similar repertory, was held several days later, on 22 March, and Chopin's farewell concert, his last in Poland, took place on 11 October 1830. Each of the young virtuoso's recitals attracted an audience of several hundred.

Warsaw: Salons

THE INFLUENCE EXERTED on the young Fryderyk's artistic awareness by the Warsaw salons of the first half of the nineteenth century seems not altogether appreciated. After the first public recitals by the little Fryderyk, the news of his extraordinary talent went around the capital's artistic environment. Salon proprietors sought to have Chopin perform during the gatherings they organised. As soon as he entered the room, he was immediately requested to perform one of his compositions or to improvise, usually on a theme put forward from the audience. The young virtuoso's brilliant displays made a great impression on listeners, as is testified by numerous accounts of his performances in the letters and diaries of those who frequented the salons of Warsaw in the early nineteenth century.

~ Probably in the home of Konstantowa Wolicka, daughter of the Margrave of Kermançon, Chopin played as a ten-year-old in the presence of the famous singer Angelica Catalani, who, enthralled by the talent of the young pianist, presented him with a gold watch, together with a dedication. He could also be seen in the aristocratic salons of the Zamoyskis, Czartoryskis and Sapiehas, as well as the Skarbeks' home. It is very likely that in 1825, in a concert at the Warsaw home of Duchess Ludwika Czetwertyńska, he was first heard by Duke Antoni Radziwiłł, who later invited Chopin to his Antonin estate.

~ Also mentioned in the Chopin literature are his frequent and important perform-

▲ Potocki Palace [Pałac Potockich]
on ul. Krakowskie Przedmieście

ances in private concerts at the homes of the
Cichowskis, Duke Maksymilian Jabłonowski,
the widow of General Sowiński, Mrs Grabow-
ska, Teresa Kicka and Klementyna Hoff-

▲ Brühl Palace, lithograph
by Schuster (J. V. Fleck),
first half of 19th c.

manowa, née Tańska, as well as the salons of the Chopins' friends, the Wodzińskis,
and, hitherto overlooked in the subject literature, the Chodkiewiczes.[22] Chopin
himself enthuses in his correspondence about taking part in the 'Fridays' chez
Kessler. These celebrated musical gatherings attracted many outstanding Warsaw
artists, who performed together in then fashionable chamber repertory. Fryderyk
related to Tytus Woyciechowski in a letter of 20 October 1829 that Kessler 'gives at
his home little musics. Everyone gathers there and plays – nothing is pre-arranged,
only what comes up in the company, that is what's played.'[23]

~ Chopin was an occasional guest at the **Belvedere** and at **Brühl Palace**,[24] a building situated between the Saxon Garden, ul. Fredry and ul. Wierzbowa, at the invitation of Grand Duke Constantine. Also considered in the subject literature is the
very likely possibility that Chopin performed at the nearby Kossowski Palace:[25]
'The plan is ready for a forthcoming soiree at the Lewickis', as Fryderyk wrote
without undue enthusiasm to Tytus Woyciechowski in a letter of 10 April 1830.[26]

~ Another notable venue was Potocki Palace [Pałac Potockich] on ul. Krakowskie
Przedmieście.[27] In a residence belonging around the turn of the eighteenth and
nineteenth centuries to Stanisław Kostka Potocki and his wife Aleksandra Potocka,
one of the most famous aristocratic salons in Warsaw was held. This was not a
typical society salon, devoted exclusively to the aristocracy. Its frequent guests
included almost all the outstanding figures in the cultural and political life of
those times. The Potockis were patrons of the arts and valued the company of

artists most highly. It is likely that the most brilliant Warsaw pianist of the day was also among their number.

~ In the Chopin literature, the Potockis' salon is enumerated among those venues at which Chopin performed, although his correspondence contains no unambiguous mention of him having played there. Since his childhood Chopin was connected with the social circle centred around Julian Ursyn Niemcewicz, who lived at the Potockis' residence. Thus there is much to suggest that he was a regular guest in this sumptuous residence, particularly after returning from his journey to Berlin. As we know, in the years 1828–30 he led a particularly active social life. During this period the salon of Aleksandra Potocka was famed for the Polish and French theatre spectacles produced there. It is doubtless one such production that Chopin laconically mentions in a letter to Tytus Woyciechowski of 27 March 1830: '[Max] was at the theatre chez Mrs Potocka'.[28]

Warsaw: Churches

THE CHURCH OF THE HOLY CROSS on ul. Krakowskie Przedmieście, next to Czapski/Krasiński Palace, where the Chopins lived, was the largest church in Warsaw at the beginning of the nineteenth century. In the Holy Cross parish Fryderyk's two sisters were baptised: Izabela and Emilia. National-patriotic ceremonies were held here, including the exequies for Prince Józef Ponia-towski. It was from here that the cortège left for Bielany following the funeral mass for Stanisław Staszic, with the young Fryderyk Chopin among the large number of Varsovians assembled to see the great scholar off to the place of his burial.[29]

~ Inside the Holy Cross church are numerous epitaphs and plaques commemor-ating great Poles, including Adam Mickiewicz, Juliusz Słowacki, Józef Ignacy Kraszewski, Bolesław Prus and General Władysław Sikorski. There is also the urn containing the heart of Fryderyk Chopin, which, in accordance with the composer's wishes, was brought to Poland by his elder sister, Ludwika. Following various twists of fate, it was transferred permanently to the Holy Cross church, as is recorded on a plaque with the inscription '17. X. 1945 the heart of F. Chopin returned to Warsaw', set into the church's second pillar, on the left-hand side of the nave. A plaque funded by the Warsaw Music Society was unveiled in 1880. It carries a quotation from the Gospel according to St Matthew (VI.21): 'For where your treasure is, there will your heart be also'. Above this is a small bust of the composer by Leonard Marconi.

◄ Church of the Holy Cross

~ The church was heavily damaged during the war, but the urn with Chopin's heart and the nineteenth-century plaque had been hidden away (see Milanówek).
~ The other churches which Chopin attended or may have frequented were also situated on ul. Krakowskie Przedmieście. On days when there was no Mass in the church of the Nuns of the Visitation, Chopin's mother would take the young Fryderyk to the Carmelite church. Attendance at Mass was obligatory for pupils of the Lyceum and students of the University. The Bernardine church of St Anne was attended, along with all female pupils, by Konstancja Gładkowska, and also—possibly on her account—by Fryderyk.

Warsaw:
Augsburg Evangelical Church
of the Holy Trinity
[Kościół ewangelicko-augsburski
Świętej Trójcy]

IN THE CHURCH that stands on what is now Plac Małachowskiego, Chopin performed for the Tsar in May 1825, playing on the aeolomelodicon, an invention by Karol Fidelis Brunner. Alexander I showed his appreciation by presenting Chopin with a diamond ring.

~ The church was built in the eighteenth century to a design by Szymon Bogumił Zug. This monumental, classicist building has the form of a domed rotunda. Its interior is circled by a two-storey gallery, typical of Evangelical churches. For some time the building, with its characteristic dome, was the tallest building in Warsaw.
~ Bombed in September 1939 and burned down during the Warsaw Rising, it was completely destroyed. The building's post-war reconstruction faithfully restored the original architectural design. Due to its exceptional acoustic, the Augsburg Evangelical Church of the Holy Trinity has been used to the present day as the venue for numerous concerts. In 1998 a new German organ was installed, founded by the National Lutheran Evangelical Church of Hanover.

◀ Augsburg Evangelical Church
of the Holy Trinity

Warsaw: Church of the Nuns of the Visitation [Kościół Wizytek]

F RYDERYK ATTENDED the church of the Nuns of the Visitation on ul. Krakowskie Przedmieście in his secondary-school years on Sunday services for pupils and students, and also after the year 1825, when he often improvised on the organ there. Writing to Jan Białobłocki in November 1825, he expressed his contentment: 'I've become the school organist. Thus my wife, as well as all my children, must respect me for two reasons. Ha, Good Sir, what a man am I! The first person in the whole school after the Revd parish priest! […] I play once a week, on Sundays, at the Visitandines' on the organ, and the others sing.'[30]

◄ Church of the Nuns
of the Visitation

▼ Church of the Nuns
of the Visitation, after a water
colour by Z. Vogel, 1785

~As a student of the High School of Music, Chopin took part in numerous performances given by the orchestra, choir and soloists of the Conservatory under the direction of the vice-chancellor Józef Elsner. Concerts were organised mainly during religious festivals and academic Sunday masses that were obligatory

for pupils of the Lyceum and students at the University. Sessions of the University Senate were also held here.

▲ Historical organ in the church of the Nuns of the Visitation

~ Already in the seventeenth century a wooden chapel stood by the entrance to the king's summer residence. A church and convent were built to a design by Karol Bay for French nuns brought to Poland by Maria Ludwika Gonzaga. Their appearance was completed by modifications made in the eighteenth century. The church's baroque façade is adorned by splendid sculptures by Jan Jerzy Plersch, who also created many elements of the rococo interior decoration, including the boat-shaped pulpit. Preserved to the present day is the historical organ on which Fryderyk Chopin used to play.

~ In the 1980s a monument was raised on the square in front of the Visitandines' church to the Primate of the Millennium, Cardinal Stefan Wyszyński, the work of Andrzej Renes.

~ Chopin's close and enduring links with the church of the Visitandine Sisters are commemorated by a plaque situated above the church doors, near the entrance to the chancel, founded by the Fryderyk Chopin Society in 1990. This bears the following inscription: 'In honour of Fryderyk Chopin, who played on the organ in this church as a pupil of the Warsaw Lyceum in the years 1825–1826'.

Warsaw: Cafés

O N UL. MIODOWA, besides numerous bookshops and musical instrument shops, there were also cafes frequented by Chopin. Opposite Brzezina's music store, in Tepper Palace on ul. Miodowa (plot no. 495), the café Pod Kopciuszkiem [Cinderella's] was in business during the years 1826–30. This functioned as a theatre café. In its tastefully furnished interior, the older generation of artists and musicians, including Ludwik Osiński and Karol Kurpiński, would gather over excellent coffee. The discussions on art that flourished here were dominated by ideas informed by classicism and French tragedy.

∼ On the entresol of the same mansion was the Dziurka [Little hole] café. Most numerous among its regular clientele were young men, chiefly the Romantic literati fascinated by Goethe, Schiller and Mickiewicz. Chopin would come here in the company of Maurycy Mochnacki, Bohdan Zaleski and Antoni Edward Odyniec.

∼ Another nearby establishment was the Honoratka, situated in an annexe of the old Zadzikowski (Chodkiewicz) Palace on the corner of ul. Miodowa and ul. Kapitulna, named after its then proprietor Honorata Zimerman; this still functions today, although a different atmosphere now reigns here.

∼ The café Pani Brzezińska [Mrs Brzezińska] (also known as U Brzezińskiej), situated near the Saxon Post Office on ul. Kozia, in the house on the corner with ul. Krakowskie Przedmieście, was, thanks to its excellent location, one of the busiest establishments in Warsaw. Chopin appeared here almost daily.

▲ Building of the Public Prosecutor's Office of the District and of Appeals and the building which housed the once legendary Pani Brzezińska café

Warsaw: Bookshops

L OCATED ON UL. MIODOWA (plot no. 481) was the bookshop and music store of Antoni Brzezina, one of the places in Warsaw most often visited by Chopin. In a letter to Tytus Woyciechowski of 3 October 1829, he wrote: 'I go to Brzezina's every day'.[31]

~ Here he regularly stocked up on sheet music and books. In a room adjoining the bookshop stood a piano, on which he readily played through his new works. Chopin published several of his works through Brzezina's lithographic press.

~ Also on ul. Miodowa, in a building later known as Kronenberg House (plot no. 486 B), Karol Ludwik Magnus had his music store and musical instrument shop.

~ Another place doubtless visited by Chopin on his way along ul. Miodowa was the music store of Franciszek Klukowski (plot no. 489), which sold exclusively music-related items, mainly sheet music and instruments.

~ He also doubtless made purchases in the Dal Trozza bookshop on ul. Senatorska (plot no. 496), in the Fine Arts store of the Frenchman Poirié situated in Krasiński Palace, where the Chopins rented an apartment, and also in Natan Glücksberg's bookshop 'under the pillars' on ul. Miodowa, as well as in the Piarist printing press, where books were not only published, but also sold.

~ Fryderyk spent long hours in the best Warsaw piano manufacturer's of those times—Buchholtz's on the corner of ul. Mazowiecka and ul. Świętokrzyska (plot no. 1352). There he tried out the new instruments and also had good conditions for playing through works he had composed for two pianos. Buchholtz could surely not have wished for a better advertisement of the instruments produced in his workshop than the recommendation of the most wonderful pianist in Warsaw at that time.

◄ *Ulica Miodowa 1777*, with Tepper Palace,
B. Belotto (Canaletto)

Warsaw: Post Office

S ITUATED IN THE ROCOCO Wessel Palace, on the corner of ul. Kozia, ul. Trębacka and ul. Krakowskie Przedmieście, was the royal post office, also known as the Saxon Post Office. The palace itself was built in the mid eighteenth century and originally belonged to General Franciszek Jan Załuski; it functioned as the seat of the post office from 1780.

~ Attached to the post office was a station from which parcels were dispatched and stage coaches departed. It is often mentioned in the literature that it was from here that on 2 November 1830 Chopin set out on what would be his farewell journey from Poland. It appears that he did indeed send out his baggage from here on that day and also bade farewell to his nearest and dearest. Fryderyk's final farewell with his friends, however, took place at a post-house in the Wola district on the city boundary.

◄ Building of the Public Prosecutor's Office of the District and of Appeals (formerly the Saxon Post Office)

Warsaw: Wileński Hotel

C HOPIN CERTAINLY VISITED the Wileński Hotel on ul. Bednarska at least once, when, in the spring of 1830, he was invited by the famous singer Henriette Sontag, while she was performing in Warsaw. Chopin, like everyone, was fascinated by the singing and the person of this exceptional artist, and he attended all her concerts in the city, including her last, on 31 May 1830 at the Royal Castle.

Warsaw: Walks

O N THE BASIS of information contained in the correspondence of Chopin and people connected with him, as well as in diaries and memoirs, it is possible to attempt a reconstruction of Chopin's daily walks around Warsaw.

▲ Plac Krasińskich, view of ul. Długa (with the then Augsburg Evangelical Church of the Holy Trinity)

~ As a child he already knew the area around Warsaw University like the back of his hand. The favourite place for little Fryderyk and his friends to play was the nearby 'Botanika', the park on the scarp behind Casimir Palace, and also ul. Oboźna, which in winter changed into a steep icy slope.

~ He probably knew every building on ul. Krakowskie Przedmieście, beginning with the newly erected Staszic Palace, where the Society for the Friends of Learning had its seat, through the area around ul. Kozia, on which stood the post office and his favourite café Pani Brzezińska, to Sigismund's Column [Kolumna Zygmuntowska], near which—in the 'ex-Cistercian' building—the Conservatory was situated. He doubtless strolled around the Old Town and visited his friends on Podwale, including Józef Reinschmidt.

View over the Bielany district
of Warsaw from the River Vistula,
M. Fajans after F. Skarbek,
first half of 19th c.

~ Doubtless one of the routes he most often took was that from ul. Krakowskie Przedmieście, in the vicinity of the National Theatre, located at that time on Plac Krasińskich. In Chopin's day, ul. Krakowskie Przedmieście and ul. Miodowa were linked by a connecting tenement house known as Roesler House. Along ul. Miodowa and ul. Długa were shops with musical instruments and the cafés Pod Kopciuszkiem [Cinderella's], Dziurka [The little hole] and Honoratka, as well as his favourite bookshop and music store, Brzezina's. The Chopins' friends, the Wodzińskis, lived in the same building as the Pod Kopciuszkiem.

~ His bosom friend Tytus Woyciechowski probably stayed in Chodkiewicz House on ul. Miodowa when in Warsaw. Maurycy Mochnacki lived on ul. Długa, with Joachim Lelewel opposite.

~ From this area it was not far to ul. Świętojerska, which he doubtless walked along when visiting the New Town, where lived his friend Alfons Brandt and also Romuald Hube, of whom Fryderyk was very fond.

~ On longer expeditions in the direction of the Żoliborz and Bielany districts he would usually be accompanied by Tytus Woyciechowski, visiting Leopold Poletyłło in the Piarist school in Żoliborz.

~ With Marceli Celiński he often followed a route leading from ul. Nowy Świat in the direction of Plac Trzech Krzyży. On ul. Marszałkowska, meanwhile, he would visit the Pruszak family.

~ Chopin also frequented the area of his first apartment, on Plac Saski, where, from the Evangelical church, then the highest building in Warsaw, he would admire the view over the city. He was also often on ul. Mazowiecka, where the piano maker Buchholtz had his establishment, as well as ul. Senatorska, at the homes of Philipeus and Odyniec, and ul. Bielańska chez Kajetan Koźmian.

~ These descriptions represent only an attempt at indicating the parts of the capital most frequently visited by Chopin. In spite of the fact that few of the original nineteenth-century buildings of Warsaw have survived to the present day, routes that follow in the composer's footsteps will doubtless prove interesting.

▲ Ulica Krakowskie Przedmieście

Warsaw: Farewell to Warsaw

◄ Fryderyk Chopin at the piano, pencil drawing by E. Radziwiłł, 1829

A T THE POST-HOUSE by the custom's house on the boundary of Warsaw, in the Wola district of the city (now 56 ul. Połczyńska), Fryderyk bade farewell to his friends, who, led by Professor Elsner, surprised him with a rendition of a farewell cantata composed specially for the occasion. Here, on 2 November 1830, Fryderyk boarded the stagecoach heading in the direction of Poznań.

~ On 2 November 1999, a plaque commemorating the composer's departure from the city was set into the front wall of what was then Primary School 306, at 56 ul. Połczyńska. Its inscription reads as follows: 'Here, on 2 November 1830, Fryderyk Chopin bade farewell to his friends, leaving his home and Poland for ever'.

Warsaw: Powązki Cemetery [Cmentarz Powązkowski]

POWĄZKI is the oldest and most beautiful cemetery in Warsaw. Founded in 1790 next to the Church of St Charles Borromeo, it became the place of rest for many eminent Poles. Sources relate that Chopin also wished to be buried at Powązki, but he had a foreboding that, for political reasons, his wish would not be fulfilled.

~ Among the graves at Powązki Cemetery are those of the family, teachers and friends of Fryderyk Chopin. The ashes of his parents, Justyna, née Krzyżanowska (1782–1861), and Mikołaj Chopin (1771–1844), which until 1948 lay in the catacombs, are now located in plot 9-IV-1, next to the grave of Stanisław Moniuszko.

~ The first member of the Chopin family to be buried in Powązki was the composer's youngest sister, Emilka (1812–1827), who died of tuberculosis aged fourteen, a few years before Chopin's departure from Poland. The Chopins' eldest daughter, Ludwika Jędrzejewiczowa (1807–1855), was buried in the Jędrzejewicz

◄ Powązki Cemetery

▼ Grave of Chopin's parents in Powązki Cemetery

TU SPOCZYWA
S.P. ANTONI FELIKS
BARCIŃSKI
PROFESSOR MATEMATYKI I FIZYKI
UR. 8 CZERWCA 1803 R. + 9 MAJA 1878
Z MAŁŻONKĄ
S.P. IZABELLA Z CHOPINÓW
BARCIŃSKA
UR. 9 LIPCA 1811 R. + 3 CZERWCA 1881 R
S.P. MARYA EUGENIA Z MAURELÓW
BARCIŃSKA
UR. W TOULUZIE 1819 R. + 6 LIPCA 1882 R.
S.P. JAN BARCIŃSKI
URODZONY 9 MAJA 1816 R.
ZMARŁ 26 KWIETNIA 1884 R.
PROSI O MODLITWĘ

W BOGU CO WIDZENI

◄ Barciński family tomb
in Powązki Cemetery

family tomb, to which Emilka's remains were also transferred from their previous resting place. The Jędrzejewicz family tomb is situated in plot 175-II-6/7. Izabela Barcińska, née Chopin (1811–1881), lies with her husband, Antoni Feliks Barciński (1803–1878), in the Barciński family tomb at II-II-9/10.

~ Buried in plot no. 159-V-1 is Chopin's teacher, Józef Elsner (1769–1854), vice-chancellor and professor of Warsaw Conservatory, composer and conductor. His grave is adorned with a statue of a Weeping Muse, made in 1855 by Wojciech Świecki to a design by Ignacy Gierdziejewski. Chopin's first teacher, Wojciech Żywny (1756–1842), lies in plot no. 12-II-20.

~ In a corner tomb, situated on the extension of the catacomb avenue, in plot no. 173-VI, is the grave of Count Fryderyk Skarbek (1792–1866), professor of political economics and administrative sciences of Warsaw University, historian and social activist, pupil of Mikołaj Chopin, with whom the Chopin family long maintained very close contacts.

~ Powązki is also the last resting place of admirers, popularisers and outstanding performers of Chopin's music. They include Jerzy Żurawlew (1887–1980; 1-I-4), Zbigniew Drzewiecki (1890–1971; 73-III-2), Mateusz Gliński (1892–1976; catacombs opposite 12-IV) and Władysław Kędra (1918–1968; Avenue of the Meritorious [Aleja Zasłużonych] 250/105).

Warsaw: Ostrogski Palace
[Pałac Ostrogskich]

Ostrogski PALACE, also known as Gniński/Ostrogski Palace, stands at 1 ul. Okólnik. From 1954 to 2005 the building was the seat of the Fryderyk Chopin Society (TiFC), which carried on the work of the Fryderyk Chopin Institute (IFC), founded in 1934. It now houses the Fryderyk Chopin Museum, for which the Fryderyk Chopin Institute (Narodowy Instytut Fryderyka Chopina) is preparing a new, specially-designed, highly modern display covering almost all the floors, from the top right down to the splendid historical vault (which is to include a concert hall), to be opened in 2010.

~ The construction of the palace, conceived as a fortified building, was commenced towards the end of the sixteenth century by Janusz Ostrogski, Castellan of Cracow. Yet the building was only erected in the second half of the seventeenth century, thanks to the then proprietor of the land, Jan Gniński. He entrusted the construction work to the Dutch architect Tylman van Gameren, who gave the design its final form. The palace was rebuilt several times, and also changed owners. During World War Two, it was almost completely destroyed. Its reconstruction was completed in 1954. The eighteenth-century-style interior was finished according to a design by Mieczysław Kuźma.

~ The museum collection can be divided into several groups: personal objects of Chopin's, manuscripts of letters (the largest collection of Chopin's correspondence in the world) and compositions, printed and handwritten documents, iconography (the famous portraits of Chopin by Eliza Radziwiłł, Maria Wodzińska and Teofil Kwiatkowski, as well as town views), sculpture and medallic art, and also extensive documentation of the International Chopin Competition. One particularly valuable item among the group of Chopin souvenirs is a grand piano by the French firm of Pleyel, on which the composer played during the last two years of his life.

Kowalewo

A T KOWALEWO, Chopin stayed in the manor house of Count Ksawery Zboiński, a relative of the Dziewanowskis of Szafarnia. Kowalewo was a base for the journey to Gdańsk which Fryderyk probably made in 1827. ~ Chopin thus characterised the atmosphere at Kowalewo in his correspondence: 'It's now morning, 8 o'clock [...] the air is fresh, the sunshine lovely, the little birds are chirping, the stream is dry, or it would be murmuring, but there is a pond and the frogs sing prettily.'[32]

~ It is not known how the Zboińskis' home looked. Preserved at Kowalewo to the present day is only the manor house (situated most probably in the same place as its predecessor) erected in 1859 for Antoni Jabłoński, to whom Kowalewo belonged in the years 1854–1891.[33]

▲ Kowalewo manor

The hamlet of Kowalewo is situated several kilometres from Drobin in Płock county.

Worth seeing in the area:
▶ Parish church of St Stanislaus the Martyr, in Drobin, with the Renaissance gravestones of the Krzyńskis.
▶ Kuchary manor, in which Helena Mniszek lived and wrote, now the property of the Karma Kagyu Buddhist Centre and a meeting-place for Buddhists from all over Europe.

Płock

Ł OCK WAS THE FIRST CITY on the itin-
erary of Chopin's planned trip to Gdańsk
in 1827. Although the city did not lie

▲ Płock, water colour
by N. Orda, first half of 19th c.

exactly along the route of the trip, Fryderyk visited it for the sake of the historical buildings there. It may be assumed that Ksawery Zboiński of Kowalewo showed
Chopin the historical centre of the city.

~ In Płock, Chopin doubtless visited the mediaeval castle walls, with their two
towers, and the cathedral, beautifully situated on a hill over the Vistula, with its
royal chapel, in which was placed, in 1825, the sarcophagus containing the remains
of two rulers of Poland, Ladislaus Herman and Boleslaus III the Wry-mouthed,
designed by Zygmunt Vogel. He may also have been interested in the historical
bell tower, the Benedictine monastery, the Dominican church and also Płock post
office, in which he expected to pick up a letter from his family.

~ The basilica cathedral, erected in the years 1126–41 by Bishop Aleksander of
Malonne, rebuilt during the Renaissance (1531–34) and restored in neo-Roman-
esque style around the turn of 1902–03, is a valuable treasure of Polish architecture. Standing in the cathedral vestibule is a copy of the famous Romanesque
Płock Door, made for the basilica c.1154 in Magdeburg. In front of the cathedral

▲ Clock Tower in Płock

are the walls of the former Benedictine monastery and the remnants of the castle built by King Casimir III the Great—two gothic towers: the Clock Tower (thirteenth-fourteenth century, fulfilling the function of the cathedral bell tower) and the Noble Tower (fifteenth century).

~ Chopin may also have visited the new Płock town hall, built in the years 1824–27 to a design by Jakub Kubicki. This was recently modernised, at the same time as the Market Square was rebuilt. The town hall has served as the seat of the city's administration since its construction.

~ Also characteristic of the landscape of the charming Vistula Valley city of Płock is the neogothic monastery of the Old Catholic Mariavite Church, erected in the early twentieth century.

This historical city, now the seat of a county administration, lies in the Mazovia voivodeship. Płock is one of the oldest and most important cities in Mazovia.

Rościszewo

THE ESTATE IN ROŚCISZEWO on which Fryderyk stayed in the summer of 1827, together with Count Zboiński, was one of the stops on his journey to Pomerania. There, before continuing the journey, he attended Sunday mass in the village church. The church of the Care of St Joseph, built in the years 1779–81, was founded by General Benedykt Jeżewski, and it still stands today.

~ Preserved to the present day is the eighteenth-century single-storey manor house with two annexes—the former seat of the Jeżewski family, the owners of Rościszewo. The house was rebuilt several times in the nineteenth and twentieth centuries.
~ The land of Rościszewo and the surrounding area contains flat arable fields, a forest, meadows and the River Skrwa Prawa, which issues from Skrwileński Lake and is a habitat for beavers. Besides houses and farm buildings, the village also contains a primary and gymnasium school, a library and Communal Council Offices.

◄ Rościszewo manor

◄ Church of the Care
of St Joseph in Rościszewo

Rościszewo is situated 10 km north of Sierpc, in the Mazovia voivodeship.

Worth seeing in Sierpc:
▶ Mazovia Countryside Museum—an open-air ethnographic museum extending over 60.5 hectares within the town boundaries, on the River Sierpienica, where it flows into the Skrwa,
▶ town hall on the Market Square; now the seat of the Mazovia Countryside Museum,
▶ Kasztelanka mansion,
▶ parish church of SS Vitus, Modest and Crescence,
▶ historical Benedictine Sisters' convent and Church of the Assumption of the Blessed Virgin Mary with a gothic figure of the Madonna and Infant.

Sanniki

C HOPIN SPENT THE MONTHS OF JULY AND AUGUST 1828 with his
school friends Konstanty Pruszak and his sister Olesia on the Pruszak family
estate in Sanniki. This village is situated 30 km north-west of Sochaczew,
and so along the route that Fryderyk took several times when travelling, for example, to Dobrinland. This beautifully situated, extensive estate belonged to
Aleksander Pruszak, who inherited it from his uncle, Castellan Tomasz Pruszak.[34]
The palace was concealed among splendid old trees.

~ In Sanniki, Fryderyk and his friends spent their time making music, playing and
walking around the shady park, as well as paying visits to neighbours and making
trips around the area.

~ Sanniki Palace acquired its present form in 1910, under the initiative of Stefan
Dziewulski, to a design by Władysław Marconi. The palace stands on ul. Warszawska
in a park surrounded by a white wall. Set into the front wall of the palace tower (in
1925, by the then owners of the estate, Antonina Maria Dziewulska, née Natanson,
and Stefan Dziewulski) is a marble plaque with the following inscription: 'In this
manor house Fryderyk Chopin stayed in 1828'.

~ In 1981 a Fryderyk Chopin Memorial Centre was created in the left wing of the
palace. Gathered here are nineteenth-century exhibits, reproductions of portraits of the composer and prints of nineteenth-century Warsaw. The interior
decor was designed by Marek Kwiatkowski, custodian of the Royal Baths Park
in Warsaw. This part of the palace also contains a
120-seat concert hall, in which 'word-and-music'
concerts have been held every first Sunday of the
month, from February to October, since 1981. The
Centre was founded at the initiative of local cultural
activists and the administration of the state-owned farm which from 1948 was
responsible for Sanniki Palace. The venture was realised thanks to collabor-
ation between the local authorities and the Fryderyk Chopin Society in Warsaw.

◄ Sanniki Palace

~ In 1985 a bronze statue of Chopin by Ludwika Kraskowska-Nitschowa was
unveiled. Situated on a marble base in front of the palace, on the left-hand side, it
depicts the composer wrapped in an overcoat, walking in a park.

~ On the first floor of the palace is the Mateusz Gliński Music Library, established
in 1986. A book collection donated by this Chopin scholar's widow, Zofia Glińska,
contains publications concerning the life and work of Fryderyk Chopin and
studies by Mateusz Gliński himself, as well as encyclopaedias, books on music
history in various languages and a collection of periodicals.

~ Besides its devotion to Chopin, Sanniki is ▲ Interior of Sanniki Palace
distinguished by its thriving folk culture, repre-
senting a distinctive subregion of Mazovia, known as the Gąbin-Sanniki region.
Still today, traditional decorations are manufactured in this area: paper-cuts,
paper flowers, painted eggs and 'pająki'—hanging ornaments of straw and tissue
paper. Each year, on the first Sunday in June, the Sanniki Sunday folk festival is
held. The cultivation of local traditions is supported by the Communal Cultural
Centre, which organises regional education and also exhibitions and markets of folk art.
~ Almost exactly opposite the main gate leading down the chestnut avenue to the
palace, on ul. Warszawska, is the Church of the Holy Trinity. In front of the church
stands a Madonna, erected in 1946 from funds raised by parishioners and thanks to
the efforts of Fr Piotr Mika. Behind the church extends a picturesque prospect over
the fields and neighbouring hamlets.
~ When visiting Sanniki, it is worth taking in the neighbouring communes of
Gąbin, Słubice, Iłów and Kiernozia, for the landscapes, the old oaks and willows
and also the nineteenth-century thatched cottages in nearby Lwówek. Some of the
villages in the surrounding area could certainly have been visited by Chopin during
his summer stay in Sanniki, and the composer travelled through Iłów and Gąbin on
his way to Szafarnia in 1824 and 1825.

▲ Sanniki Palace

Sanniki, in Gostynin county, lies 86 km from Warsaw, in the Mazovia voivodeship.

Worth seeing in the area:
► Gąbin town hall,
► monuments of nature in Iłów,
► parish church of St Margaret in Kiernozia,
► classicist Łączyński Palace, set in historical grounds in Kiernozia. The history of this property is connected with the fortunes of Fryderyk Chopin's father, Mikołaj. Around the turn of the eighteenth and nineteenth centuries, the widow Ewa Łączyńska employed him at Czerniewo (part of the Kiernozia estate) as tutor to her children. We may assume, therefore, that the excellent French of Maria Walewska (née Łączyńska), admired by Napoleon, was to a considerable extent the work of her good teacher—Mikołaj Chopin.[35]

Sochaczew

T HE ROUTE TO SZAFARNIA, where Chopin spent successive summers in 1824 and 1825, led along the road from Warsaw through such places as Błonie, Sochaczew and Płock, and almost every stay at Żelazowa Wola included walks and trips to neighbouring towns and villages. Thus Fryderyk could have been a regular visitor to nearby Sochaczew.

~ From letters to Tytus Woyciechowski, we learn that during his final visit to Żelazowa Wola, in the summer of 1830, Fryderyk accompanied Michał Skarbek on a trip to Sochaczew. Stationed there, in command of the 3rd Infantry Brigade, was General Piotr Szembek, a great music lover and accomplished violinist. Planned at that time were further meetings in Sochaczew to play music together, but these plans were not realised before Chopin's departure from Żelazowa Wola. However,

◄ Ruins of the Castle of the Mazovian Dukes in Sochaczew

▲ Ruins of the Castle of the Mazovian Dukes in Sochaczew, lithograph by K. Stronczyński

shortly after his return to Warsaw, on 29 August 1830,[36] Fryderyk received a surprise: a carriage was sent for him from the camp of the 3rd Infantry Brigade at Sochaczew. Chopin wrote of this in a letter to Tytus Woyciechowski: 'Also, I was lately in Gen. Szembek's camp once again. I should tell you that he always holds court in Sochaczew and he agreed with Michał that I would be taken to him. When, however, this did not come about, he sent his aide [...] Czajkowski and they took me to him there.'[37]

~ General Szembek's camp was probably set up in the former Dominican Sisters' convent near the old Castle of the Mazovian Dukes, or, more precisely, its ruins. At the military camp to which Fryderyk was taken post-haste, the regimental band played for him (to his approval, and even admiration), and the commander himself also showed his skills on the violin.

~ Chopin, meanwhile, played his own compositions, including the Adagio from the F minor Piano Concerto. When the musical displays had ended, Fryderyk was driven back to Warsaw. From the letter in which he described the whole event to Tytus, we learn that he still managed to make it to an opera that evening at the National Theatre. The spontaneity of this situation is more in keeping with present-day realities than with the accepted standards of two centuries ago; it was undoubtedly a somewhat surprising, yet pleasant, event for the young man.

~ The building of the Dominican Sisters' convent was destroyed during World War Two, whilst the ruins of the castle on a hill in Sochaczew remain perfectly visible today from the main road leading through the town.

~ Sochaczew honoured Chopin with an obelisk and a bust of the composer, unveiled in 1961 in the park on ul. Warszawska and ul. Romualda Traugutta; it bears the inscription 'Fryderyk Chopin 1810–1849'.

Sochaczew is a county town on the River Bzura, around 60 km from Warsaw.

Worth seeing in the area:
▶ Museum of the Sochaczew Region and of the Battlefield on the Bzura and also the Narrow-gauge Railway Museum in Sochaczew,
▶ Classicist manor house in an old park in Czerwonka; now home to a State Primary and Secondary School of Music,
▶ Franciscan Fathers' monastery at Niepokalanów.

▲ Mazovian landscape
near Żelazowa Wola

～ The most important Mazovian locations connected with Chopin are Żelazowa Wola, Brochów and Sanniki. Today, in these three villages Chopin is worshipped and his memory cherished; the same is not true, however, of Rościszewo and Kowalewo, referred to by Fryderyk in a letter to his family, the inhabitants of which have long since forgotten about those brief, yet documented, episodes in the composer's life.

～ Doubts may be raised regarding his supposed visit to the family of Eustachy Marylski in Książenice or Pęcice,[38] places in which his sojourn is merely hypothetical.

Milanówek

MILANÓWEK, SITUATED NEAR WARSAW, between Brwinów and Grodzisk Mazowiecki, is an important place connected with the composer's memory. In the period from 9 September 1944 to 17 October 1945, on the first floor of the presbytery of St Jadwiga's church in Milanówek, in the private chapel of Archbishop Antoni Szlagowski, an urn containing Fryderyk Chopin's heart was kept. It had earlier been removed by the Germans from the Church of the Holy Cross in Warsaw, and then, in the presence of witnesses, presented to Archbishop Szlagowski by the German general Erich von dem Bach-Zelewski. In 1986 a plaque commemorating this incident was installed near the entrance to the presbytery, blessed by Archbishop Jerzy Modzelewski, who was present when the urn was handed over. The plaque bears the following inscription: 'In this presbytery an urn containing the heart of Fryderyk Chopin was kept from 9. IX. 1944 to 17. X. 1945'.

~ During the ceremonial celebrations of the seventieth anniversary of the parish of St Jadwiga, in 1998, a bust of the composer was installed in front of the presbytery. Placed on the base was a plaque with the following inscription: 'In commemoration of the stay of the urn containing the heart of Fryderyk Chopin in the parish of St Jadwiga in Milanówek in the years 1944–1945, founded through the efforts of the Milanówek Cultural Society and the donation of Joanna and Andrzej Nowak of Milanówek. June 1998'.

▶ Mazovian landscape

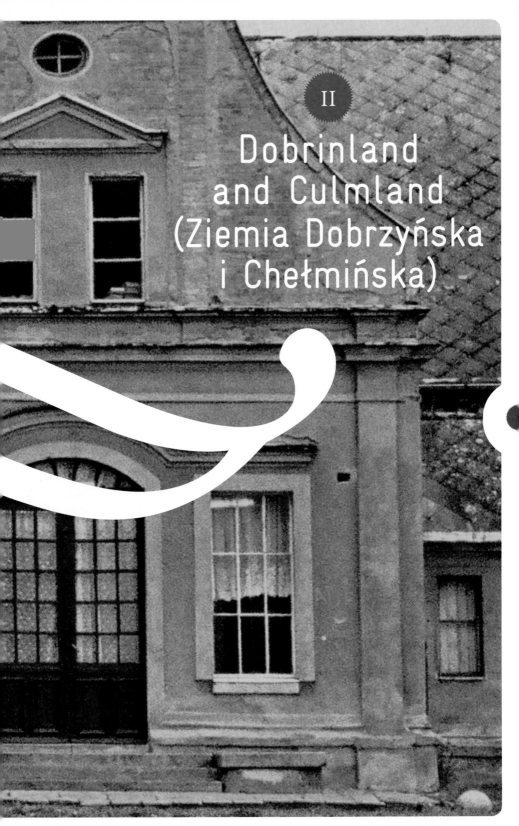

II

Dobrinland
and Culmland
(Ziemia Dobrzyńska
i Chełmińska)

Szafarnia

F RYDERYK COMPLETED HIS FOURTH YEAR OF SECONDARY SCHOOL with a performance in a public display of pupils' talents. The event was re- ported by the *Gazeta Korespondenta Warszawskiego i Zagranicznego* (no. 128 of 1824), which listed the pupils' names. He was also awarded a distinction: 'Mori- bus et Diligentiae/Federici Chopin/in Examine Publico/Lycei Varsaviensis/Die 24. Juli 1824'. This dedication was embossed in gold letters on the cover of the book which he received as a prize.[39]

~ Towards the end of July 1824, Fryderyk set off on a long-awaited holiday for the Dziewanowski family estate at Szafarnia. The proprietor of the village and grange of Szafarnia[40] at that time was Julian (Juliusz) Dziewanowski,[41] father of Dominik, known as Domuś. Since 1822, Domuś had been a pupil of the Warsaw Lyceum, a school-friend of Fryderyk, and he boarded with the Chopins. The boys became friends and, after a successful end to the school year, in the summer of 1824 (most probably under the care of Ludwika Dziewanowska, Domuś's aunt) they left on their holidays for Szafarnia. Chopin stayed on this beautifully situated estate in Dobrin- land until September. It was a real country holiday, with his hosts taking care to en- sure the young Chopin of every possible amusement, although without dispensing him from the household customs. Besides a great deal of free time spent playing with Domuś, numerous walks and trips in the surrounding area, Fryderyk also had time to practise, or rather to play for pleasure, not infrequently four-handed with Miss Ludwika. The young man tried to remember about caring for his fragile health, which was rather good at this time.

◀ Szafarnia Palace

~ The details of this sojourn in Szafarnia and, of most value to posterity, Fryderyk's own impressions from this wonderful holiday are perfectly documented thanks to the extensive, extremely detailed accounts of his stay in Dobrinland, abounding in anecdotes and apt observations, contained in his *Kuryer Szafarski*. Here is an extract from the 'Home News' section, carrying in- formation intended for his family, concerning Fryderyk's amusements and daily life, reports of musical events, and also characteristic observations on the Szafarnia fauna, from an account dated 16 August 1824:

~ 'On 11 August this year his lordship Fryderyk Chopin took a ride on a plucky mount and competed to the line: and though, several times proceeding on foot, he was unable to rival Mrs Dziewanowska (in this, not he, but his horse bore the blame), he nevertheless gained victory over Miss Ludwika, who, already quite close to the line, arrived on foot. – His lordship Franciszek Chopin rides out daily on walks, yet with the honour of always sitting behind.'

~ 'His lordship Jakób Chopin drinks six cups of acorn coffee a day, whilst Mikołaiek eats four rolls each day, *nota bene* besides a mighty dinner and three-course supper.'

~ 'On day 13 of the current month and year His lordship Better could be heard on the piano with uncommon talent. A virtuoso, this Berliner – plays in the taste of HL Berger [...] in the thrust and set of his fingers surpasses Mrs Łagowska and plays with such feeling that almost every note seems to come, not from his heart, but out of his mighty belly.'

~ 'On day 15 c. m. & y. the important news arrived that a baby turkey had happened to hatch in a corner behind the pantry. An important incident this, in that, not only did it cause the family of turkeys to increase, but it also increased the tax revenue and ensured its continued augmentation.'

~ 'Last night a cat stole into the wardrobe and smashed a bottle of juice; but just as on the one hand apt for the scaffold, on the other it also merits praise, as it chose the smallest among them. – On 12th inst. a hen fell lame and a drake lost a leg in a duel with a goose. A cow fell so violently ill that she even grazes in the garden. – On 14th inst. the sentence fell that, under pain of death, no piglet should dare enter the garden.'[42]

~ The summer Chopin spent around Szafarnia was a great success. Thanks to Domuś and Jan Białobłocki, from Sokołowo, Fryderyk was assured of excellent company in all amusements, and also companions for music. The climate of Dobrinland proved beneficial to his physical and mental state. After such a splendid holiday, there was no doubt as to the plans for his next vacation. Fryderyk spent the following summer in Szafarnia as well.

~ The history of the estate of Płonne, of which Szafarnia was originally part, has been associated with the Dziewanowski family since the first years of the eighteenth century.[43] The Szafarnia manor was situated within the area of Sokołowo Forest, abounding in pines and oaks. Around its inhabited part, the forest changed into a park, containing a garden, orchards and two small ponds. Next to a vegetable garden stood the timber manor house where the Dziewanowskis lived. Domuś's father was owner, not only of Szafarnia, but also of nearby Płonko,[44] which Juliusz Dziewanowski inherited from his father in 1815. He then moved to Działyń, transferring the estate, in 1838, to his son Dominik. The Dziewanowskis' old timber house, where Chopin stayed, was pulled down in 1910, at the request of Szafarnia's new owner, Feige, who erected a walled house, probably in a different place to the old building. The mansion and what remained of its outbuildings were then taken over by the next proprietors, the Noskowskis.

~ Today, the mansion is home to a Chopin Centre, equipped with concert hall and small museum. The building is set in a three-hectare park with six natural monuments (including the 'Chopin linden' and 'Dziewanowski oaks'). The small annexe to the right of the mansion was most probably already standing at the time of Chopin's sojourn in Szafarnia.

~ The idea of commemorating Chopin's stay in Szafarnia and initiating cultural activities there, particularly concerts, arose on 17 October 1949, on the centenary of the composer' death. Near that date, on 25 September 1949, the first Chopin Festival was organised, combined with the exhibition Around Chopin, devised by Professor Mieczysław Tomaszewski, which included works (drawings and sketches) by the Kotlarczyk brothers of Toruń, depicting the places visited by the composer in the years 1824–25. The festival was accompanied by a concert given by Stanisław Szpinalski, Irena Jęsiakówna and the Pomerania Symphony Orchestra under the direction of Arnold Rezler. At that time, a Fryderyk Chopin Memorial Room was set up in the mansion at Szafarnia. Three years later, on 7 September 1952, a commemorative plaque was unveiled, which proclaims: 'In Szafarnia and the surrounding villages Fryderyk Chopin stayed in the years 1824–1825. In the eighth year of the existence of the People's Poland, the School in Szafarnia was named after him. 1952.'

~ The plaque was set into the front wall of the mansion, which at that time also housed a primary school. During this ceremony the Memorial Room was renamed the Centre of the Cult of Fryderyk Chopin. In that same year the Fryderyk Chopin Society donated to the Centre several exhibits (including reproductions of the *Kuryer Szafarski*, copies of the composer's manuscripts, a portrait of Chopin, a plaster bust, and casts of his hand and death mask).

~ In the years 1957–77, the Centre was known as the Music Salon. Between 1970 and 1976 the Centre's activities were suspended. A fire in 1979 consumed part of the roof and an upstairs room; many exhibits were destroyed, and the Music Salon was flooded with water. In the years 1980–88, the Centre's work was suspended once more, and the mansion's renovation was not completed until 1988. The F. Chopin Cultural Centre, as it was now renamed, renewed its activities on 10 September; the opening ceremony was accompanied by an exhibition of traditional embroidery and sculpture and a concert given by the Baltic Philharmonic's wind quartet, Ewa Pobłocka and Igor Śmiałowski. At that time, the Centre gained new rooms appointed with stylish furniture. The first floor of the mansion was converted into a primary school. The cultural and artistic work commenced at that time has continued to the present day.

~ Today, the Centre organises concerts, music workshops and masterclasses, *plein-air* painting workshops, reciting and art competitions, exhibitions, tournaments of knowledge about Chopin, New Year balls, and above all the Fryderyk Chopin International Piano Competition for children and youngsters, which has been held since 1993. In May 2001 a bronze bust of Chopin on the front wall of the mansion, made to a design by Roman Dantan, was ceremonially unveiled. In the years 2001–03, the Chopin Centre at Szafarnia was beset by numerous problems. In 2002 the Radomin Communal Council passed a resolution to close down the primary school on the first floor of the mansion, and in 2003 to close down the Centre itself. This led to efforts to protect the Chopin heritage, successfully concluded in 2004. In the years 2005–2006 the palace underwent a general refurbishment. The Centre now has a number of extra facilities: three practice rooms, an audiovisual room for 40 people, four guest rooms and a cafe.

~ In Płonne, preserved to our times are the old manor park (near to the school) and the gothic church from the turn of the fourteenth and fifteenth centuries, together with the obelisk in memory of the war hero Jan Dziewanowski (1782–1808), a 'fearless knight', commander of 3 Company of the 1st Regiment of the Light Cavalry of the Guard, who fell in the charge at Somosierra in Spain. Standing nearby is a classicist bell tower from the first half of the nineteenth century.

Szafarnia and Płonne are located in the Radomin commune, in Golub-Dobrzyń county, respectively 7 km and 9 km from Golub-Dobrzyń itself.

Worth seeing in the area:
▶ commemorative plaque to Maria Dąbrowska on a stone near the primary school in Płonne. The writer stayed there for four years (1925–28), gathering material for her novel *Nights and Days*,
▶ fifteenth-century gothic church in Radomin (constructed from erratic blocks),
▶ baroque church in Dulsk from the second half of the eighteenth century,
▶ beech avenue and landscape park in Radomin (natural monument),
▶ larch hill in Płonne (natural monument).

Around Szafarnia

URING THE SUMMER MONTHS, Fryderyk stayed not only in Szafarnia itself. He was a frequent guest on neighbouring estates. In the aforementioned *Kuryer Szafarski*, modelled on the popular Warsaw daily *Kuryer Warszawski*, he enumerates the places with which he became acquainted, including Płonko, Dulnik, Białkowo, Golub, Lipno and Nieszawa.

~ Together with the Dziewanowskis, he was invited by the Wybranieckis to Sokołowo. The company doubtless called on the Cissowskis of Radomin and Rętwiny, and also the Piwnickis—proprietors of the estates of Gulbiny and Płonne. In Ugoszcz and Obory lived the Borzewskis, in Bochenie the Ciżewskis, and in Obrowo the Romockis. There were many families of the landed gentry related to, or friendly with, the Dziewanowskis in the surrounding area. And so (as in Warsaw), families readily invited the talented pianist to their properties, to bring variety to his sojourn in Dobrinland and also in the hope that the music of the already famous young virtuoso might resound in their homes. All of these locations and names can be found in Chopin's correspondence with his family, in which Frycek, as editor 'Pichon' (Cho-pi-n), with the permission of the 'Censor', incarnated by Ludwika Dziewanowska, relates the anecdotic 'Home News' and 'Foreign News'.

~ Unfortunately, the original walls of most of the manors visited by Chopin have now disappeared without trace, although the mansion in Ugoszcz in which Chopin was a guest has survived.

▲ Landscape
   of Dobrinland

Ugoszcz

▲ Ugoszcz Palace

T HIS PROPERTY ORIGINALLY BELONGED TO THE HOUSE OF ZIELIŃSKI, of the Świnka coat-of-arms, and then from the end of the eighteenth century to the Borzewski family visited by Fryderyk. The guests from Szafarnia were doubtless received by the then owner, Antoni Borzewski.

~ Located in Ugoszcz (situated in the commune of Brzuze, in Rypin county) is a well-preserved, eclectic-style palace from the nineteenth century. For some time it was home to a primary school, and now houses the Kombatant Welfare Home. It is set in an old park with historic tree stand and a characteristic eighteenth-century rococo gate. To the left of the palace stand the farm buildings, and behind it lies a lake.

~ The history of such places as **Płonko**, **Płonne** and **Bocheniec** are strictly related to the above-described fortunes of Szafarnia, since they were part of the Dziewanowskis' estate. In **Gulbiny** a ruined manor house still stood until the 1950s. It may be assumed that this was the same building in which the Piwnickis once received the young Chopin.

Gulbiny

I N GULBINY, ON LAKE DŁUGIE, there once stood a manor and park. The ruined building was demolished in 1959. The older inhabitants of Gulbiny remember its appearance: a thatched timber manor house with porch and walled elements. Today, no trace remains of the house, although there are parts of the park, with an ancient wood and part of the old layout. It was founded some two hundred years ago by Alojzy Piwnicki, and the last owners were Bolesław Brzezicki and Helena Brzezicka, née Piwnicka, who were murdered by the Germans in their home (as were many other local landowners).

Gulbiny and Ugoszcz belong to the commune of Brzuze, next to Radomin, in Rypin county. The landscape of this area is varied, with many hills and lakes but a relatively small amount of woodland.

Worth seeing in the area:
- mediaeval emplacement ruins at Żałe ('Kopiec'), Somsiory ('Szaniec') and Kleszczyn,
- sanctuary of the Holy Family in a pilgrimage chapel from 1704, with a miraculous spring, at Studzianka,
- Trąbin parish church, from 1881,
- chapel at Ostrowite, from 1930 (dedicated to the memory of combatants in the Polish-Bolshevik War),
- nineteenth-century manor house at Ostrowite.

Obrowo

▲ Obrowo manor

ONE IMPORTANT LOCATION IN CHOPIN'S CORRESPONDENCE, referred to many times, was Obrowo, belonging at that time to the House of Romocki—the family of Józefa, the future wife of Dominik Dziewanowski.

~ It is highly probable that around fifteen years after Fryderyk's summer holidays in Szafarnia, his sister Ludwika spent some time in Obrowo. The following appears in a letter she wrote to her brother in October 1842:

~ 'My dearest Fryderyk,

A week ago today I returned from a three-month journey around the world; I spent two months in Ciechocinek, where the children were on a cure, and one at the home of the Romocki family, and I visited the whole Dziewanowski family, young and old. They speak warmly of you wherever I go. The benches you made in Szafarnia are no longer there, only imitations with pleasant memories of you.'[45]

~ The composer himself begins his account in the *Kuryer Szafarski* as follows: 'On the 20th inst. the harvest festival was held in Obrowo. The entire village gathered in front of the manor house was engaged in whole-hearted amusement, especially after vodka, and the girls sang out in a shrill voice, a semitone out'.[46]

~ The fourteen-year-old Chopin's stay in Obrowo certainly made a great impression on him. It is probably here that he first encountered the rural music of

Dobrinland, listened to bands and ditties, and saw the regional dances. A year later, on 26 August 1825, in a letter to his parents written from Szafarnia, he gave an extensive and extremely colourful account of the harvest festival. From this we learn that the composer not only listened in on the merry-making that crowned the harvest, but took an active part: he played on the bass and even danced, which gave him a great deal of joy.

~ Preserved in Obrowo is the manor house where Fryderyk Chopin was a guest of Hieronim Romocki. The brick building was built around the turn of the eighteenth and nineteenth centuries, and then slightly modified in 1898. Its first recorded owner was Jan Romocki (second half of the eighteenth century).

~ Today the house is the seat of the Communal Offices, the Registry Office, the Communal Council and the Enterprise Support Centre. Situated near the manor is a small park with old tree stand, including European ash, blue spruce and black locust. At the initiative of the teacher and artist Michał Kokot, chairman of the Osiek Folk Culture Association, a plaque was set into a wall of the building reminding visitors of the composer's sojourn in the hamlet. The plaque, unveiled on 6 August 2004, reads: 'In this manor house, in 1824 and 1825, Fryderyk Chopin stayed and performed, also taking part in the local harvest festival, or "okrężne"'.

Obrowo is situated in Toruń county, on both sides of the DK10 road.

Worth seeing in the area:
► Church of St Lawrence (with two rococo side altars from the second half of the eighteenth century) in Dobrzejewice,
► parish church (with baroque font from the seventeenth century) in Osiek nad Wisłą,
► parish church from 1848 and classicist manor house in Łążyn,
► mansion and park in Zębowo,
► nineteenth-century peasant cottages ('Dobrzynki').

Obory

DURING HIS HOLIDAYS IN SZAFARNIA, Chopin is certain to have had the opportunity to visit the Carmelite monastery, strongly connected with the Dziewanowski family, which supported the monastery financially for several generations.

▲ Interior
of the church
in Obory

~ Built four hundred years ago, at the initiative of a Mr and Mrs Rudzowski, for Carmelite Fathers brought here specially, was the first timber church, located atop the Grodzisko hill (now known as Kalwaria). Barely a few years later, the church was burned down in a fire, and in its place, in 1617, the Carmelites began constructing a new timber church, which they built over the next ten years, ultimately converting it into a walled edifice.

~ The building of the walled church in Obory dates from the years 1627–1642. In the mid eighteenth century, during further rebuilding work, a quadrangle tower 45 metres high was erected. Today, the baroque church of the Discalced Carmelite Fathers contains many valuable items, including numerous altars and the chapel of Providence. Revered for centuries is a miraculous figure of Our Lady of the Seven Dolours (the 'Pieta Oborska'), which was made from lime around the turn of the

◄ Church in Obory

fourteenth and fifteenth centuries. Also preserved in the church is the organ on which Chopin is supposed to have played.[47]

～ The monastery of the Discalced Carmelites in Obory, adjoining the church, was built in the years 1741–53. Alongside, on the Grodzisko hill, stands an historical cemetery and chapel of the Holy Cross, erected in 1686 and rebuilt in the nineteenth century. Below the monastery and cemetery is the monastery garden with a Way of the Cross.

～ In order to commemorate Fryderyk Chopin's sojourn in Obory, in 1999 a plaque was installed in the church, with the following inscription: 'In Obory church in the summer of 1824 Fryderyk F. Chopin spent some time and played on the organ'. The church contains epitaphs to the members of families that were friendly with the Chopins, including Teresa Zboińska (d. 1827), Ludwik Borzewski, judge of Dobrinland (d. 1807), Salomea Borzewska, née Nałęcz (d. 1833), and Stanisław Piwnicki, Speaker of the House of Deputies in 1825 (d. 1840).

Obory lies in the commune of Zbójno, in Golub-Dobrzyń county. It is a hamlet with an exceptionally picturesque landscape, hence the name 'Dobrzyń Switzerland' that is often used. The eastern and central parts of the commune of Zbójno lie within an area of protected landscape, due to the unique Zbójno Drumlins, a group of mounds with streamlined shapes, extended in the direction of the motion of a glacier. These mounds are separated from one another by narrow depressions, in which small ponds and lakes occur. The commune also contains the Działyńskie-Wielgie lake complex and the River Ruziec.

Worth seeing in the area:
▶ Działyń church, from the beginning of the seventeenth century,
▶ mansion-park complexes in Zbójno and Wielgie.

Golub

▲ Golub-Dobrzyń Castle

ONE OF THE MORE IMPORTANT of the numerous excursions from Szafarnia connected with visits to nearby estates was the trip to Golub.

~ Golub is traversed by the River Drwęca, which in Chopin's times also constituted a state border, dividing the Prussian Golub from the Russian Dobrzyń.

~ Fryderyk doubtless visited the fortified castle on a hill above the town, probably also the nearby Renaissance church of St Catherine and other spots in this interesting small town. He mentions this in his *Kuryer Szafarski*, writing in the 'Foreign News' section: 'On the 26th inst. his lordship Pichon was in Golub.'[48] However, this is unlikely to have been Fryderyk's only excursion in the area of Golub-Dobrzyń.

~ Situated on a hill in Golub was a timber stronghold, on the site of which, during the times of the Teutonic Knights, a gothic fortified construction was raised at the initiative of Commander Konrad von Sack. The castle was erected around the turn of the thirteenth and fourteenth centuries and rebuilt in the fifteenth century.

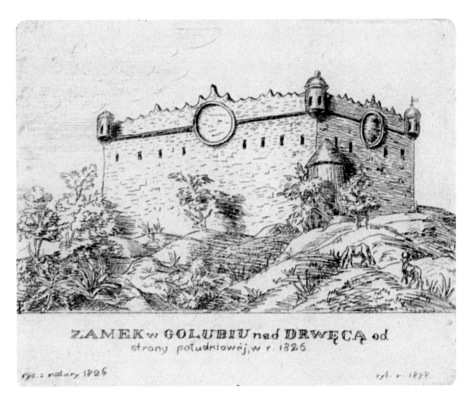

ZAMEK w GOLUBIU nad DRWĘCĄ od
strony południowej, w r. 1826

rys. z natury 1826   ryt. r. 1838

▲ Golub-Dobrzyń Castle
on the River Drwęca,
aquatint by T. Żebrowski, 1826

It changed hands several times, alternately stormed by the Poles or regained by the Teutonic Knights.

~ In the seventeenth century, following further modernisation in a late Renaissance style, during which new living quarters were built onto the castle, it became the favourite residence of Anna, sister of King Sigismund III Vasa. According to historical sources, this period was particularly prosperous for both the castle and the town, over which the princess extended her protection and her rule, favourable to the local population. As a result, in Golubian legend she has remained the good spirit of the castle ever since. From the mid nineteenth century the castle was deprived of a good owner for over a century and fell into considerable decline, until renovation work completed in the 1960s restored the walls to their splendid appearance of old. The composer probably visited the castle—Golub's principal attraction—with Ludwika Dziewanowska, as is mentioned by a chronicler writing under the pseudonym Józef znad Drwęcy.

~ Since 1951 the town has carried the name Golub-Dobrzyń, as a result of the joining together of Golub and Dobrzyń, situated on either side of the River

▲ Moat around
Golub-Dobrzyń Castle

Drwęca. Held in the castle, picturesquely situated on a hill (Chełmno Uplands), are a range of events, the most famous being the Grand International Knightly Tournament. The town is also home to a Regional Museum, an armoury, a school of chivalry and a hotel.

Golub-Dobrzyń is situated about 40 km north-east of Toruń.

Worth seeing in Golub-Dobrzyń:
► gothic church of St Catherine from the fourteenth century, with its characteristic, majestic tower and baroque interior,
► tenement house from 1617 (with mannerist gable) and timber house from the second half of the eighteenth century on the market square,
► classicist church from 1823,
► Evangelical church from 1909 (now a primary school).

Sokołowo

ON THE BASIS of a number of reliable sources, mostly from Chopin's corres-pondence, we may conclude that during his time at Szafarnia Chopin visited his friend Jan Białobłocki at Sokołowo. At that time, Sokołowo was in the possession of Jan's step-father, Antoni Wybraniecki, the second husband of Katarzyna Monika, née Zbijewska. Numerous mentions of Fryderyk's stays at Sokołowo can be found in his friends' voluminous youthful correspondence.

~ Announcing an imminent visit to his friend in a letter of 17 July 1825, Chopin writes: 'Once I get to your home, I'll explain to you that riddle', adding towards the end of the letter the famous exclamation: 'Ah, I could just smell Sokołowo!'.[49] In spite of the examination that awaited him the following day, he was already joyfully anticipating the approaching holiday. In the same letter, Fryderyk confesses to Jan that were it not for the plans of his companion, Ludwika Dziewanowska, he would like to visit Sokołowo before arriving at Szafarnia.

▲ Sokołowo manor

~ In another letter, probably written in Sokołowo towards the end of a summer spent in Dobrinland, he confessed with bitterness: 'I promised to be at your home yesterday, but could not make it to Sokołowo until today. [...] you'll not believe how sorry I am, how very sorry I am!... So much so, that I don't want to leave. Why did I struggle all the way here by britzka when I found no-one in, but at least you will know that I was here. That I was here, so as to bid you and your papa a fond farewell.'[50]

~ Chopin's friendship with Jan Białobłocki, five years his senior, dated from the times when the Chopins ran a boarding home in Casimir Palace. Białobłocki was a pupil of the Warsaw Lyceum and then went on to study law at the University. However, his regular studies were complicated by a quickly advancing illness, which forced him to take numerous cures. After leaving Warsaw, Jan spent most of his time on the family estate of Sokołowo. Chopin endeavoured to provide his friend with all the news from Warsaw and also keep him up to date with new music publications. Their correspondence, carried on quite regularly during this period, ended suddenly in 1828. Jan Białobłocki died from tuberculosis aged barely twenty-three.

~ A later manor house, known as the 'hunting lodge', now stands in Sokołowo. This is managed by a State Treasury Company, which cultivates the land and runs an Animal Husbandry Centre (pheasant and partridge).

The commune of Golub-Dobrzyń lies among picturesque lakes, including Grodno, Słupno and Owieczkowo. It includes numerous forest complexes. Sokołowo is situated barely 4 km from Golub-Dobrzyń.

Turzno

D URING HIS SECOND SUMMER spent in Dobrinland, Fryderyk made several excursions further afield. One of these was a trip to Turzno, in Culmland.

~ 'Tomorrow morning we set off for Turzno, and we are not to return until Wednesday', wrote Fryderyk from Szafarnia to his parents on 26 August 1825.[51]

~ This was a trip beyond the Dobrinland boundary, and also beyond the then Prussian-Russian border. Although this area lay at that time under Prussian administration, the estate to which Chopin set off from Szafarnia was a real traditional Polish manor and a bastion of patriotism. It contained a rich art collection and an excellently equipped library. Doubtless there was also no lack of a good instrument—a clavichord or possibly even a piano.

~ Since the 1730s, the estate had been in the possession of the Zboińskis, who built at Turzno a mansion in classicist style. From the beginning of the eighteenth century, these lands were owned by Augustyn Bartłomiej Działowski,[52] who, together with his family, received the young virtuoso from Warsaw towards the end of summer 1825[53]. The details of Chopin's stay in Turzno are not known. All we do know is that the visit lasted several days.

▲ Turzno Palace

~ Available sources relating to the history of Turzno,[54] and also studies devoted to places visited by Chopin in the north of Poland and in Prussian lands, contain references to a second visit to Turzno. This visit is linked to the composer's travel plans, specified in a letter to his parents of 6 July 1827, written from Kowalewo, near Płock: 'When we're leaving for Płock, it would be madness on my part not to mention it. So today in Płock, tomorrow in Rościszewo, the day after tomorrow in Kikół, a couple of days in Turzno, a couple of days in Kozłowo and the next moment in Gdańsk, and back again.'[55]

~ Since Fryderyk's previous stay, serious changes had taken place in the Działowski family: the previous year Augustyn Działowski had died. His widow, Katarzyna Działowska, née Jeżewska, now lived in the Turzno mansion with her two daughters, Józefa and Julianna, whilst her son Ksawery had become independent, taking over the family estate of Mgowo. Thus, there is no certainty as to the number of visits made by Chopin to Turzno. However, distinguished in the composer's correspondence, it was unquestionably marked by his presence.

~ What is now the main palace in Turzno was erected in the mid nineteenth century on the site of its predecessor, which had been founded by Augustyn Działowski. Both the palace itself and the castle-style garden bower, or pavilion, were designed by Henryk Marconi. In the first half of the twentieth century the Gajewski family added the palace's left wing. An avenue of chestnut trees leads from the entrance gate to the palace complex. Extending alongside the palace is a landscape garden of several hectares with an old tree stand, the oldest specimens being two plane trees, a European beech and a pedunculate oak. From 1947 the complex housed a primary school, and before that was the seat of the Toruń School of Horticulture. Today, the palace and its grounds are the property of the firm Arpol.

◄ Ruins of the bower
in the grounds of Turzno Palace

Turzno lies on the boundary of the Toruń Basin and Culmland (also known as the Chełmno Lake District), in the commune of Łysomice, Toruń county, less than 20 km from Toruń. Among the commune's geographical features are the picturesque Kamionkowskie Lake and the Piwnicki Forest nature reserve.

Worth seeing in the area:
▶ gothic-style church of St Nicholas (renovated in 1882) in Papowo Toruńskie,
▶ sixteenth-century gothic church of the Assumption of the Blessed Virgin Mary in Gostkowo.

Toruń

I N THE MIDDLE OF THE SUMMER of 1825, Fryderyk, on his second holiday at Szafarnia, sent to his friend Jan Matuszyński a humorous description
of his impressions from a recent visit to Toruń:[56] 'What on earth did you see
in Puławy?[57] You saw but a small part of that which my eyes beheld in full. After
all, you saw in Sybil's Temple a brick taken from the home of Copernicus, from the
place of his birth? But I saw the whole house, the whole place, albeit now somewhat
profaned. Just imagine, dear Jasiu, in that corner of the room where this famous
astronomer was gifted with life, stands the bed of some German, who doubtless,
after stuffing himself with spuds, occasionally breaks quite frequent zephyrs, and
more than one bug wanders around those bricks of which one was sent with great
ceremony to Puławy. Thus, my brother, a German pays no heed to who lived in this
house; he allows himself a whole wall of such profanation as Duchess Czartoryska
would not permit herself a single brick.'[58]

~ However, as it later turned out, the house (on the corner of ul. Kopernika and
ul. Piekary, now a tenement house at 40 ul. Kopernika) over the poor state of which
Fryderyk so lamented, was, up until the 1880s, erroneously identified as the birthplace of the great astronomer.[59]

~ The historical buildings of the fortified city of Toruń made a great impression
on Fryderyk:

◄ Old Town Wall in Toruń

'That is all that I am able to write to you about
Toruń, I might tell you more, but only this will I
write, that the greatest impression [...] was made
on me by the gingerbread. I have seen, it is true,
all the fortifications from all sides of the city, with all the details, I saw the famous
machine for moving sand from one place to another [...] besides this churches of
gothic construction, founded by the Teutonic Knights, one of them built in 1231. I
saw the leaning tower, the famous town hall, both outside and inside, the greatest
peculiarity of which is that it has as many windows as there are days in the year, as
many halls as months, as many rooms as weeks, and that its entire edifice is most
magnificent, in the gothic taste. Yet all of this does not surpass the gingerbread, oh
that gingerbread, a piece of which I've sent to Warsaw.'[60]

~ In Toruń, Chopin could admire the specific, highly diversified architecture, including the mediaeval burgher buildings—the granaries and also the gothic town
hall (Fryderyk's description of which is not entirely accurate). He also mentions
the splendid churches standing in the vicinity of the town hall. It is very likely,
therefore, that he visited the three gothic churches. In addition, he saw that unique
Toruń attraction, the Crooked Tower, dating from the beginning of the fourteenth
century, part of the city's gothic defence system—a 'must-see' for all tourists.

◄ Crooked Tower in Toruń

~ But his tour of the city was dominated by the gingerbread, that true Toruń treasure. Earlier in the same letter he wrote the following: 'But Copernicus aside, I shall start writing about the Toruń gingerbread. In order that you might know it well, and perhaps better than Copernicus knew it, I shall convey to you an important item of information relating to it, which may serve for some of your scribblings; the information is as follows. According to the local bakers' custom, the gingerbread shops consist of hallways piled up with well-locked chests, in which the sorted gingerbread, arranged in dozens, lie. You'll doubtless not find this in Adagiorum Hiliades [sic], but knowing your curiosity in such weighty matters, I report it to you, that you be able to cope, when translating Horace, with dubious, tortuous meanings.'[61]

~ Fryderyk had many reasons to be particularly interested in visiting various parts of this beautiful city. The family of the Chopins' good friend, Professor Samuel Bogumił Linde, was connected with Toruń, where Chopin most probably stayed in the tenement house of the Fenger family. This was a splendid eighteenth-century building formerly belonging to Jakub Fenger, father of Countess Ludwika Skarbek. It was here, in 1792, that Fryderyk Skarbek—regarded by Chopin's family as Fryderyk's godfather—entered the world.

~ To commemorate the composer's stay in Toruń, a plaque was set into the wall of the Fengers' house (at 14 ul. Mostowa), which reads: 'In this house Fryderyk Chopin stayed in the year 1825'.

~ Below this is another plaque: 'In this house lived Fryderyk Skarbek 1792–1866, an eminent penitentiary, economist, historian and man of letters. On the centenary of his death—ZSP Toruń.'

▲ Toruń—view from the east,
lithograph by J. G. Bach
after a design by R. Assmus, *c.*1860

Toruń lies on the River Vistula, which divides the city into two uneven parts (the larger part on the north bank). Toruń, like Turzno, is situated in Culmland and constitutes a sort of boundary between the historial regions of Cuiavia and Pomerania, yet for historical and administrative reasons it is officially part of Pomerania.

Kikół

I N A LETTER DATED 6 JULY 1827,[62] written from Kowalewo to his family in Warsaw, Chopin lists the places where he planned to stop on his journey to Gdańsk. Still today, it has not been established with the utmost certainty with whom Fryderyk made this journey. After visiting Rościszewo (described in length in the subchapter devoted to Mazovia), he stopped at the estate of Karol Zboiński in Kikół.

~ Count Karol was the only son of Ksawery Zboiński[63] and most probably inherited the Kikół estate on his father's death, in 1818. Chopin, resting on his way to Pomerania, spent here several days, about which no detailed information has come down to us.

~ Kikół is a village situated in the vicinity of picturesque lakes. Towards the end of the eighteenth century, a splendid two-storey palace was erected for the House of Zboiński[64] on a small elevation. Built on a rectangular plan, in classicist style, the eighteenth-century building remained in good condition until World War Two,

▲ Kikół Palace

► Landscape of Dobrinland

when it was heavily damaged. It was rebuilt in the years 1952–64. Among its finest features is a Knights' Hall (with polychromes from the turn of the eighteenth and nineteenth centuries). The garden surrounding the palace was laid out in the first half of the nineteenth century. After 1945 it went to ruin, but was later restored to its former glory. During the second half of the twentieth century the building was home to a holiday-training centre. Today, the palatial complex is in private hands.

Kikół lies in Dobrinland, on Kikolskie Lake, in Lipno county.

Most of the towns and villages of Dobrinland, also known as the Dobrzyń Lake District, currently belong to the north-eastern part of the voivodeship of Cuiavia-Pomerania. Dobrinland is delimited by three rivers, the Vistula, Skrwa and Drwęca, and its principal towns are Lipno, Rypin, Dobrzyń nad Wisłą, Skępe and Górzno. It is an exceptionally picturesque area, abounding in lakes, rivers, forests and hills, with numerous monuments of nature and architecture.

III

Silesia
(Śląsk)

Wrocław

C HOPIN VISITED WROCŁAW (Breslau, in his day) on several occasions, most probably four times. In late July and early August 1826 he journeyed to Lower Silesia with his mother, visiting the family region of his teacher, Józef Elsner. This was not an exclusively touristic jaunt; Fryderyk was to undergo a cure to improve his health. Mother and son travelled in the direction of Duszniki (Reinertz), to join up with Ludwika Skarbek, who was already in the area.

~ Along the route, which Fryderyk describes in detail (enumerating all the larger towns) in a letter sent that summer to Wilhelm Kolberg, he lists Wrocław as the twelfth 'stop' on the way. The fact that a break here from the journey was planned may be testified by the fact that Professor Józef Elsner, who had earlier been associated with this city, entrusted his pupil with letters for his friends there. Chopin discharged this task in part when he stopped overnight in Wrocław on the way to Duszniki; as he wrote, 'Mr Latzel' was very pleased at the letter. On his way back from the spa, he visited Friedrich W. Berner, organist at St Elizabeth's, and also Joseph I. Schnabel, chapel-master of Wrocław Cathedral. One may presume that Fryderyk also demonstrated to the addressees his pianistic skills.

~ It is not known whether Chopin, who was merely passing through Wrocław, managed to visit anything else besides the two churches referred to here. Of a similar character may have been his next visit to Wrocław, when three years later Fryderyk stopped here on his way back from Vienna, where he had travelled in the summer with a few friends. Only in November 1830 did he stay in the city for a longer time. On that occasion, he and Tytus Woyciechowski stayed at the Zur Goldenen Gans [The golden goose] inn on Junkernstrasse (now ul. Ofiar Oświęcimskich). In the evening of their arrival they went to the Municipal Theatre on Taschenstrasse (now at the junction of ul. Oławska and ul. Piotra Skargi) for a performance of Raimund's *Der Alpenkönig und der Menschenfeind*.

◄ Market Square and St Elizabeth's Church in Wrocław

~ Maria Zduniak writes of the two friends' stay, identifying in her article the places visited by Chopin:[65]

'On Sunday 7 November, Chopin and Woyciechowski went to Wrocław Cathedral, to meet the chapel-master and composer Joseph I. Schnabel, who, pleased at the encounter, as one may surmise, invited his guests to the morning rehearsal for the concert that was to take place on the evening of the following day in the Grand Hall of the Merchants' Club on ul. Biskupa, known at that time as the hall of the Hotel de Pologne.'

~ What subsequently occurred during the rehearsal at the Merchants' Club is best conveyed by the words of Fryderyk himself, taken from a letter to his family

in Warsaw, written in Wrocław on Tuesday 9 November 1830: 'I found there a small, as usual, orchestra that had turned up for the

▲ Wrocław Cathedral, M. Grossmann, first half of 19th c.

rehearsal, a piano and some referendary, an amateur, by the name of Hellwig, preparing to play the First Concerto in E flat major by Moscheles. Before he sat down at the instrument, Schnabel, who had not heard me for four years, asked me to try out the piano. It was difficult to refuse, so I sat down and played a couple of variations. Schnabel was infinitely pleased, Mr Hellwig got cold feet, and others began to request that I perform in the evening. More particularly, Schnabel so kindly insisted that I couldn't dare refuse the old gentleman. He's a great friend of Mr Elsner's; but I told him that I'd do it just for him, since neither had I played for a couple of weeks, nor was I intending to show off in Wrocław. To that the old man said that he knew all of this and that he had wanted to ask me yesterday in the church, but was too embarrassed. Then I went with his son to get some music and played them the Romance and Rondo from the Second Concerto. At the rehearsal the Germans admired my playing, saying "Was für ein leichtes Spiel hat er", but nothing about the composition. Tytus even heard one of them saying, "that I knew how to play, but not compose". '[66]

~ There are no detailed records of the places visited by Fryderyk and Tytus. We do know that their guide around Wrocław was 'a merchant by the name of Scharff', whom they had met by chance. An amusing situation occurred when the gentleman in question, wishing to suitably entertain the young men in his city, decided to invite them to the concert: 'The next day he signed us in at the hostel and finally fixed us up with Fremdenkarten for yesterday's concert', recalled Fryderyk in the same letter. '[…] How great must have been his […] surprise when this Fremder turned out to be the principal musical protagonist of the evening. Besides the Rondo I also improvised for the connoisseurs on a theme from *La muette de Portici*. After that they closed with a rendition of the overture, which was followed by dances.'[67]

Wrocław: Church of St Elizabeth [Kościół św. Elżbiety]

T HE HISTORY OF THIS CHURCH,[68] situated near the market square in Wrocław, dates back to the first half of the thirteenth century, as is evidenced by the preserved fragments of the walls of a Romanesque church. Saint Elizabeth was made patroness of a gothic church constructed over a period of more than one hundred years, from the first half of the fourteenth century. This church was an important cultural centre for the inhabitants of Wrocław, and over its history changed hands alternately between Protestants and Catholics. In the fifteenth century the renowned Elisabethianum gymnasium school was founded here. In addition, the church was famed for its valuable library collections of both manuscripts and printed publications. In the first half of the nineteenth century, it was a gothic church with a characteristic tower, numerous Renaissance and baroque elements, a huge collection of tombstones of deceased townsfolk from various periods, and also a valuable eighteenth-century organ. This was the largest organ in Silesia, built in the years 1750–51 by Michał Engler. It is very possible that Chopin had the good fortune to hear the sounds of this famous instrument, and perhaps he even played on it himself during his visit to Friedrich Berner.

▲ Market Square and St Elizabeth's Church in Wrocław, aquatint by P. P. Troschel

Wrocław: Cathedral of St John the Baptist on Ostrów Tumski Island
[Katedra Św. Jana Chrzciciela na Ostrowie Tumskim]

THE ERECTION OF THE FIRST CHURCH on this site is linked to the beginnings of the Wrocław bishopric. In the tenth century a stone pre-Romanesque building stood here. In the twelfth century a splendid Romanesque edifice, known as the Walterowska, was built in its place. During the first half of the thirteenth century it was decided to build a third cathedral on this site. After almost one hundred years' work, a gothic cathedral appeared in the landscape of Ostrów Tumski, adapting certain elements of the Romanesque construction in its architecture. The ravages of World War Two engulfed almost the whole of the cathedral, with the result that its original appearance, both inside and out, could never be fully reconstructed.

~ Among the places visited by Chopin during his several visits to Wrocław (in the years 1826, 1829 and 1830) were the Municipal Theatre (then on Taschenstrasse, now at the junction of ul. Oławska and ul. Piotra Skargi), the Grand Hall of the Merchants' Club, known at that time as the hall of the Hotel de Pologne (on ul. Biskupa), the Rautenkranz [Rue garland] inn (on ul. Oławska) and the Zur Goldenen Gans [The golden goose] inn (then on Junkernstrasse, now ul. Ofiar Oświęcimskich), which was destroyed during World War Two.[69] Chopin also visited, as already mentioned, the Cathedral of St John the Baptist, on Ostrów Tumski Island, and the Church of St Elizabeth, on ul. Św. Mikołaja.

~ In South Park [Park Południowy], founded towards the end of the nineteenth century to a design by Hugo Richter, near the junction of ul. Andrzeja Woligórskiego and ul. Powstańców Śląskich, there stands a monument to Chopin, made by Jan Kucz, portraying the composer seated in an armchair listening to music. The idea of commemorating Chopin's stay in Wrocław initially came from Maria Zduniak, and was taken up by Wojciech Dzieduszycki, long-serving chairman of the Wrocław Branch of the Fryderyk Chopin Society in Warsaw. On the front is an inscription reminding the public that Chopin performed in Wrocław on 8 November 1830. On the back is another inscription: 'This monument was built through the efforts of the Wrocław Branch of the Fryderyk Chopin Society and the Com-

mittee for the Building of a Fryderyk Chopin Monument, thanks to grants from the
Ministry of Culture, Wrocław Municipal Government, Lower Silesia Voivodeship,
Strzegom Region Stoneworkers Association, Dach Bud Ltd, Polska Miedź Founda-
tion and donations from the public. Wrocław 5 IX 2005.'

> Wrocław is the capital of Lower Silesia and one of the largest cities in Poland.
> It lies on the River Odra, in the Silesian Lowlands.

Oleśnica

~ Situated some 30 km from Wrocław is Oleśnica, mentioned by Chopin in his correspondence. The town honoured the composer's memory with a bust, placed on a
base (with the inscription 'Fr. Chopin'), in front of the historical building which is
home to the Fr. Chopin Primary School of Music and the Lower Silesia Music Society (between ul. Kościelna and ul. Matejki).

> Worth seeing in Oleśnica:
> ▶ Castle of the Dukes of Oleśnica (fourteenth-nineteenth centuries),
> ▶ gothic church of St John the Evangelist,
> ▶ remains of the town's defensive wall (fourteenth-sixteenth centuries).

Duszniki Zdrój (Bad Reinertz)

C HOPIN STAYED IN DUSZNIKI IN THE SUMMER OF 1826. On completing his final year at the Warsaw Lyceum, he went with his mother on a journey to the 'Silesian waters' for a cure, joining there Ludwika Skarbek and Emilka Chopin. The previous month, Ludwika Chopin had stayed at Duszniki Kudowa with Count Fryderyk Skarbek, his wife Prakseda, and their little son Józef.

~ We know the exact route taken on the approximately week-long journey from Warsaw to Silesia thanks to a description contained in the introduction to a letter written by Fryderyk in Duszniki to his friend Wiluś (Wilhelm Kolberg) on 18 August 1826. The route led through 'Błonie, Sochaczew, Łowicz, Kutno, Kłodawa, Koło, Turek, Kalisz, Ostrów, Międzyborz, Oleśnica, Wrocław, Nimsch, Frankenstein, Warta and Glatz',[70] and thence only some '4 miles' to Reinertz. On arrival, they took accommodation in the Dom

Duszniki—pavilion with colonnade, colour lithograph by E. Knippel, second half of 19th c.

◄ Chopin Monument in Duszniki Zdrój

Bürgla [Bürgel House] pension. In those times, this was a modern and comfortable pension, offering both accommodation and full board, with meal

▲ Hermitage
in Duszniki Zdrój

times fitted around the recommended rhythm of a guest's cure in the spa's waters.
∼ In the above-mentioned letter to Wiluś, Fryderyk ironically describes the detailed daily schedule at the spa, without omitting the various 'attractions' that were part of the town's tradition: 'In the morning, 6 o' clock at the latest, all the Ailing at the spring; here, wretched brass music compiled from a dozen or so caricatures in various tastes [...] is played to the slowly perambulating Kur-gästs [...] This promenade along the lovely avenue connecting the Anstalt with the town lasts usually until eight, depending on how many cupfuls one has to drink in the morning, then everyone (each to his own) goes off to breakfast. – After breakfast I usually go off for a stroll, walk until 12, at which time dinner must be eaten, because after dinner we go once again to the Brun. The afternoon [...] is again sullied by music, and apart from that one walks around until evening. Like me, since I drink only two glasses of Lau-brun after dinner, so I go home early for supper, and after supper to sleep.'[71]
∼ Fryderyk, somewhat bored with the walks around the spa and the daily obligation of drinking the waters (from the Laubrunn spring) with added goat's-milk whey and herbs, eagerly described his impressions and his plans for further trips into the mountains around the spa. He rued not being permitted to wander around the Sudeten mountains due to his fragile health: 'Admittedly, I do walk around the moun-

▲ Hermitage on Rozalia's Mount in Duszniki, oil painting (signed *F. W. Schwemter*), 1833.

tains by which Reinertz is surrounded, often delighted by the view of the local valleys, wandering back down reluctantly, sometimes on all-fours, but I've not yet been there, where everyone goes, as it's been forbidden me.' Meanwhile, he writes further into the letter of his plans: 'We're going to the Hohemenze, which is supposedly also a mountain in sumptuous surroundings; I'm expecting it to come about.'[72]

~ Fryderyk also mentions a remarkable spot in Duszniki traditionally visited by visitors to the spa, which appears to have been the object of a joint trip with the Skarbeks: 'Having climbed up the mountain, one of the highest in Reinertz, one walks up a hundred and several dozen steps in a straight line, almost perpendicular, made of stone, to the hermitage itself, from which there is a sumptuous view over the whole of Reinertz.'[73]

~ The expedition with the Skarbeks to the hermitage on the hill (which Chopin called Rozalia's Mount) was described, along with other details of her stay, by Chopin's sister, Ludwika, who gave a meticulous account of all the events of that summer, seen through the eyes of little Józef, the Skarbeks' small son whom she often looked

after during their stay. Thus 'Józef's journey from Warsaw to the Silesian waters', and also the diary kept during that time by Count Skarbek, entitled 'Journey to the Silesian Waters and surrounding [towns?] in the summer of 1826',

▲ Duszniki—view over the Spa Park, colour lithograph by E. W. Knippel, second half of 19th c.

became two sources of information relating to the party's stay in the spa.[74]

~ Ludwika mentions in her little tale a visit to a paper mill in Duszniki, situated on the edge of the town. It is highly likely that Fryderyk also visited this interesting factory. It is certain that he possessed paper made there, which he used for correspondence, as he emphasises in a letter to Jan Białobłocki.

~ Without doubt, the most important event during the sojourn in Duszniki should be seen as Fryderyk's performance. This fact, described a thousand times over, is shrouded in legend, as is usually the way with Chopin's performances. Silesian spas had always cultivated the proud tradition of the ubiquitous presence of music. This tradition was not always associated with a high standard of performance, and so the more demanding listeners were not always satisfied with the musical attractions offered in the spa.

~ As we learn from sources, three years prior to Chopin's stay a concert was held in Duszniki in which the main protagonist was the fourteen-year-old Felix Mendelssohn. The young pianist did without the accompaniment of the semi-amateur ensemble and decided to improvise solo on themes from Mozart and Weber. Both

▲ Chopin House in the Spa Park in Duszniki

performances, by Felix and by Fryderyk, were of a charitable character. One may assume that the young pianist was encouraged to give a recital in the spa while still in Warsaw. Yet a fundamental problem in Duszniki proved to be the lack 'of the one thing which all the beauties of Duszniki cannot replace, that is a good instrument'.[75]

˜ In spite of that, Fryderyk decided to perform. There are even hypotheses concerning two such recitals.[76] It is worth mentioning that the *Kuryer Warszawski* of 22 August 1826 included the following notice: 'when several children were orphaned by the death of their father, who had come to the waters for a cure, Mr Chopin, emboldened by persons aware of his talent, gave two concerts in aid of the children, which brought great honour to him and assistance to them.' The concert, or two concerts, was held in the hall of the Spa Theatre, built in the 1800s to a design by H. Geissler. Cultural life in the spa revolved around the 'kursal'—a small mansion in the centre of the Spa Park.

˜ In the Spa Park in Duszniki Zdrój, one of the key sites of the cult of Fryderyk Chopin in Poland, there remains much to remind visitors of his stay, including the mansion named Chopin House, an obelisk, a monument and the Pieniawa Chopina mineral water intake.

~ Particularly noteworthy is the mansion (also known as the Chopin Theatre), built at the beginning of the nineteenth century. Since 1946 an annual International Chopin Festival has been held there. Moreover, for over twenty years now, outstanding Polish and foreign piano teachers have run there master-class courses for young virtuosos from all over the world during the days leading up to the festival.

▲ Chopin House in the Spa Park in Duszniki

~ The obelisk, located near the mansion, was unveiled on 19 June 1897; it was founded by Wiktor Magnus,[77] director of the Merkury Food Association in Warsaw. A medallion bearing the composer's effigy, made from bronze by Stanisław Roman Lewandowski, was placed on the obelisk, and below this a plaque with an inscription in Latin: 'FRIDERICO CHOPINO REINERH A. MDCCCXXVI ARTE SUAVIS-SIMA, HUMANITATE EXIMIA, GENEROSAM VIRTUTIS INDOLEM INEUNTE ADOLESCENTIA TESTIFATO, HOC MONUMENTUM A. MDCCCXCVII AD REI MEMORIAM SEMPITERNAM DECURIONUM PERMISSU IMPENSA SUA POLONO POLONUS EREXIT'.[78]

~ Also standing in the Spa Park are a Chopin Monument by Jan Kucz, unveiled on 8 August 1976, and the Pieniawa Chopina (formerly Brunne) mineral water intake, located near the Pump Room.

~ The pension where Chopin and his mother stayed while in Duszniki (Dom Bürgla [Bürgel House]) stood on the site of what is now the Nokturn Holiday Home (at 6 ul. Zielona), earmarked for demolition. A plaque commemorating Chopin's stay was set into the front wall of the building, but later removed (most probably in 2004).

~ During his stay in Duszniki, Chopin is known to have walked up the steep steps to the hilltop Hermitage. This historical building has survived to the present day. For many years it housed the museum of the International Chopin Festival, but it is now under the care of the Duszniki Zdrój Youth Town Council.

Duszniki Zdrój lies in Lower Silesia, in the Kłodzko Basin, on the E67 road. Situated nearby are two other well-known spas: Polanica Zdrój (in the direction of Kłodzko) and Kudowa Zdrój (in the direction of the Czech border). The Bystrzyca Dusznicka flows through the town.

Worth seeing in the area:

▶ seventeenth-century paper mill (now a Museum of Paper-Making) on the Bystrzyca Dusznicka in Duszniki (at 42 ul. Kłodzka), on the E67.

▶ baroque church of SS Peter and Paul (with whale-shaped pulpit) and sandstone sculpture of the Madonna and Infant accompanied by SS Florian and Sebastian, made by L. Weber in 1725, both in Duszniki,

▶ gothic church of the Assumption of the Blessed Virgin Mary (fourteenth-sixteenth centuries) with baroque interior, in Kłodzko,

▶ gothic bridge (from fourteenth century) with baroque sculptures, in Kłodzko.

IV

Pomerania (Pomorze)

Pomerania

I N A LETTER DATED 6 JULY 1827, written from Kowalewo to his family in Warsaw, Chopin lists the places where he planned to stop on his journey to Gdańsk. As already mentioned, it has yet to be established with the utmost certainty that Chopin actually made this journey. If, however, it did indeed come about, then it is most probable that the young Fryderyk travelled under the care of Ksawery Zboiński of Kowalewo.[79] Scholars disagree over whether Fryderyk's company changed at different stages in this journey.[80] After visiting Rościszewo, a village situated on the border between Mazovia and Dobrinland, the next stop was Kikół, at the home of Karol Zboiński.

~Further along the route, the company stopped to rest at another friendly residence, namely on the Działowskis' estate in Turzno, and then in the homeland of Ksawery Zboiński at the estate of Kozłowo.

Kozłowo

I n what was then the province of West Prussia, not far from Świecie, in the mid eighteenth century the Zboińskis took over a splendid estate—Kozłowo. Towards the end of the century, Kozłowo covered 300 hectares and included: 'a noble property, one manor farm, a mill, distillery [and] brewery'.[81]

~During Chopin's visits, this extensive estate, inherited from members of the House 'de Kościelec et Ossówka Zboińskich',[82] was Ksawery Zboiński, also owner at that time of Kowalewo, near Płock. It was to Ksawery Zboiński that Fryderyk referred in his correspondence as 'Mr Zboiński'; and it was doubtless under his care that Fryderyk travelled in 1827 in the direction of West Prussia.

~Kozłowo was inherited from Ksawery by his eldest daughter, Julia Joanna Olimpia, who died childless in 1867. The estate then came into the possession of her youngest sister, Kamila, and then her son, Józef Turowski, the last proprietor of the Kozłowo entail estate from the Zboiński line.[83] Fryderyk may have been in Kozłowo, at the home of the Chopins' friends, the Zboińskis, at least twice. However, there is no further information on these brief visits.

~Today, nothing remains of the Zboińskis' manor house at Kozłowo. The only reminder of the composer's stay in this hamlet on the River Wda is a stone bearing a commemorative plaque, on which the inscription reads: 'In commemoration of Fryderyk Chopin's sojourn at Kozłowo and Świecie in the summer of 1825 [sic]. PTTK Świecie Branch 1985.'

◄ Pomeranian landscape

Kozłowo is located in Świecie county, Cuiavia-Pomerania voivodeship, in Pomerania, on the River Wda; it constitutes virtually a suburb of Świecie.

Worth seeing in the area:

► in Chełmno: gothic town wall (with towers), Grudziądz Gate (transformed in 1620 into a chapel), late Renaissance town hall from 1567–72 (now Culmland Museum), six gothic churches (including the churches of the Assumption of the Blessed Virgin Mary, St James, SS Peter and Paul and St John the Baptist,

► gothic church of St Nicholas and complex of port granaries from seventeenth and eighteenth centuries in Grudziądz.

Gdańsk

G DAŃSK (in Chopin's day Danzig), the most important city in West Prussia, was undoubtedly an attractive goal for a young man on a summer expedition. Chopin's sojourn in Gdańsk has long raised doubts. It is difficult to speak with any certainty of this matter, since information contained in a letter to his parents, written in Kowalewo on 6 July 1827, concerns only his plans, and not impressions from an actual visit: 'When we're leaving for Płock, it would be madness on my part not to mention it. So today in Płock, tomorrow in Rościszewo, the day after tomorrow in Kikół, a couple of days in Turzno, a couple of days in Kozłowo and the next moment in Gdańsk, and back again.'[84]

~Most scholars are of the opinion that if this trip did come about, then it took place in that month of July 1827. Also in the realms of speculation is the true motive for such an expedition. Fryderyk did not really have any close relatives or friends in Gdańsk. In earlier literature, an oft-repeated assumption is that 'the aim of Chopin's journey to Gdańsk was a wish to become acquainted with this city and also to pay a visit to Doctor J. W. Linde, a pastor attached to the Church of the Holy Spirit in Gdańsk. Dr Linde, the elder brother of the vice-chancellor of the Warsaw Lyceum, lived in Gdańsk at no. 1859 (up to 1945 no. 29, no longer in existence) ul. Tobiasza (Tobiasgasse). Chopin most probably stayed at his home when visiting Old Gdańsk in July 1827.'[85]

~Speculation regarding this visit is put forward by Andrzej Bukowski in his book *Pomorskie wojaże Chopina* [Chopin's travels in Pomerania], where he assumes that Fryderyk

◀ Gdańsk, Long Riverside [Długie Pobrzeże]

▼ Gdańsk, Long Riverside [Długie Pobrzeże], lithograph, 1825

◄ Neptune's Fountain
in Gdańsk

was part of a larger party of travellers from the Kingdom of Poland ('Count Zboiński of Świecie, Count Sierakowski of Waplewo and Count Dembowski with family'), who resided in Gdańsk from 9 to 15 August at the 3 Mohren [Three Moors] Hotel at 31 Holzgasse (now ul. Kładki). It is difficult to determine unequivocally which assumption is closer to the truth. The numerous views on this question do not provide us with an answer to the most important question: what exactly did Chopin see in Old Gdańsk? How much time did he spend there? Intuition tells us that he may have visited the main historical buildings, as well as places that were fashionable at that time. It has even been suggested, perhaps overspeculating somewhat, that Fryderyk also took in the area around Sopot and Oliwa during his maritime expedition.[86]

～ We know little about Fryderyk Chopin's visit to Gdańsk. There are, however, grounds to assume that the composer probably stayed at the 3 Mohren Hotel (no longer in existence), near the Chapel of St Anne and the Church of the Holy Trinity. He may possibly also have paid a visit to Jan Wilhelm Linde (brother of Samuel Linde) in the tenement house at 1859 (no longer in existence) ul. Tobiasza. Assuming that the Gdańsk expedition did indeed come about, Chopin would most probably have visited the Long Riverside [Długie Pobrzeże], with its Crane, and what is now ul. Długa, with its characteristic monuments and historical buildings: Artus Court [Dwór Artusa], the Church of St Mary and Neptune's Fountain.

 Gdańsk lies at the mouth of the River Motława, where it flows into the Vistula, on Gdańsk Bay and the Baltic Sea.

Waplewo

T he next port of call on 'Chopin's travels in Pomerania' was probably Waplewo, which at the beginning of the nineteenth century was certainly one of the most beautiful estates in the region. The route to Waplewo affords travellers a magnificent view of Malbork Castle. If Fryderyk did indeed journey to the Sierakowskis' estate, he undoubtedly had the opportunity to at least see the castle from the road. Chopin's host, Antoni Sierakowski, was a descendent of Wacław Sierakowski, the well-known Cracow man of letters, musician and theorist.

~At Waplewo, near Sztum, the Sierakowskis created an 'oasis', assuring themselves and their talented guests the best possible conditions for the cultivation of their art. Music was the host's great passion, and he undoubtedly had in his possession a good keyboard instrument, as well as a rich library.

~The palace, built in the first half of the seventeenth century, was surrounded by an extensive regular garden with sculptures and bowers, whilst the interior was adorned by authentic works of art and sculpture. One may assume that Antoni Sierakowski and his wife Antonina, née Zboińska, hosted Chopin for several days. There is no certainty as to where Fryderyk travelled from there: did he actually journey to Gdańsk[87] or rather make the long return journey home?

~Evidence of Fryderyk Chopin's stay in Waplewo with Antoni Sierakowski may be provided by a document from the end of the nineteenth century—a biography written

▲ Waplewo Palace

in 1889 by his grandson, Adam Sierakowski, in which we find the following extract: 'Antoni Sierakowski of Waplewo, born 19 May 1783 [...] was an art lover heart and soul, but above all a

▲ The Sierakowskis' manor at Waplewo, near Sztum, 19th c.

musician, who played very well on the violin and also composed and published a great deal. The famous composer Chopin was his friend and guest at Waplewo.'[88]
~According to Andrzej Bukowski, the composer stayed at Waplewo from 15 to 20 August 1827.[89] This is, however, merely an hypothesis, which is confirmed by no other documents. Among the guests at Waplewo were also Józef Ignacy Kraszewski, Oskar Kolberg and Jan Matejko.

~Preserved to the present day is the historical palatial complex with its grounds, the history of which dates back to the beginning of the fourteenth century. The palace was rebuilt several times during the nineteenth century. Waplewo was first owned by the House of Rab (from 1483 to the beginning of the seventeenth century). The Rabs were succeeded by the Niemojewski (1611–41), Zawadzki (1641–1710), Chełstowski and Bagniewski (1710–59) and Sierakowski (c.1760–1939) families.
~The garden was laid out towards the end of the eighteenth century by Kajetan Sierakowski, Antoni's father. Monuments from that period have survived to the present day, including the Chinese pagoda and nobleman's statue.

▲ Waplewo Palace

Among the tree stand are such monuments of nature as European beech, European ash, London plane and black walnut.

~Since 2006 the palace has been a branch of the National Museum in Gdańsk and has housed the Museum of the Noble Tradition and the Pomeranian Centre for Contacts with the Polish Diaspora.

Waplewo is situated on the DW515 road, in the county and region of Sztum, 15 km from Sztum itself, in the Cuiavia-Pomerania voivodeship.

Worth seeing in the area:
▶ fortified castle of the Teutonic Knights at Sztum,
▶ castle, fragments of town wall, thirteenth-century church of St John and gothic town hall in Malbork.

V

Greater Poland (Wielkopolska)

Kalisz

'FRYDERYK CHOPIN HAD THE OPPORTUNITY TO OBSERVE THE PROGRESS in the rebuilding of Kalisz, as he stopped here in passing six times (counting only documented visits): at the end of July and in the middle of September 1826 (journey to Duszniki), in the first week of September 1829 (return from his trip to Vienna), 21–22 October and 7 November 1829 (journey to Strzyżewo and Antonin); he also stayed there from the evening of 3 November to 5 November 1830 (stopover before leaving the country, never to return).' Thus may we list as briefly as possible, in a single breath—after Henryk F. Nowaczyk—[90]all the composer's stays in this town.

~ On at least two occasions, Fryderyk spent more time in Kalisz than the minimum required for rest during a journey. It is certain that, returning in merry company from Vienna, Chopin visited with his friends Doctor Adam Bogumił Helbich. Among the friends accompanying Chopin on that journey were Ignacy Maciejowski and Alfons Brandt. And it was with the physician's family of the latter that Doctor Helbich was closely linked. The young men arrived in Kalisz on 2 September 1829 and went straight to Helbich's home in the hope of putting up there. However, their planned stopover did not last long, as their host happened to be on his way to a wedding in Żychlin. They would certainly not have been upset at the doctor that, instead of a rest from their tiring journey, he proposed them new attractions—leaving with him for the wedding.

~ Another episode in Kalisz occurred at the beginning of November 1829, when Fryderyk stopped over there when returning from Antonin: 'On the way back I was in Kalisz at a soiree with Mrs Łączyńska and Miss Biernacka. She pulled me up to dance, I had to dance a mazur, and that with an even lovelier maid than she, or at least equally as beautiful. [...] I was in Kalisz only one day', he wrote in a letter to Tytus Woyciechowski in Poturzyn.[91]

Kalisz lies on the River Prosna, in the Kalisz Uplands. It is one of the oldest towns in Poland and the second largest town in the Greater Poland region and voivodeship, after Poznań.

Strzyżew

S TRZYŻEW[92] WAS A SMALL ESTATE situated in Krotoszyn county, in the Grand Duchy of Posen. The property of Stefan Wiesiołowski and his wife Anna, née Skarbek, Strzyżew lay near Ostrów Wielkopolski in the parish of Kotłowo, and neighboured with the extensive estate of Duke Antoni Radziwiłł. As sources are lacking in detailed descriptions of the Wiesiołowskis' estate, the laconic reference to Strzyżew in Ludwika Chopin's children's story 'Little Józef's journey from Warsaw to the Silesian waters...' takes on crucial significance.[93] From her description, we learn that the manor house (we may assume that it differed little from the manor at Żelazowa Wola) was surrounded by a cherry orchard, with raspberries and strawberries growing in the garden and also a vegetable patch. As for the interior, it would seem to have been typical of the home of a fairly wealthy family, with paintings on the walls, including portraits of the Skarbeks' ancestors; a clavichord doubtless stood in the parlour, on which the members of the household would have played. The Wiesiołowskis had four children: one daughter, the eldest of the siblings, and three sons.

~ The Chopins travelled 'abroad' to Strzyżew rather infrequently, although the routes taken by members of the family on their journeys were planned so as to stop here for a shorter or longer visit. Thus we may presume that the composer stayed in Strzyżew several times. He did not rule out visiting Strzyżew, for example, on the way back from his holiday in Vienna, in the early autumn of 1829, although we do not know if this visit came about.[94] He most probably spent a little time there over a month later, after 20 October that year.

~ It seems that Anna Wiesiołowska, as Fryderyk's godmother, was very keen on promoting the young man, already renowned for his outstanding talent. Her godson's several visits to Strzyżew afforded the perfect opportunity to acquaint him with Duke Antoni Radziwiłł.[95] Such may be testified by a passage from a letter to Tytus dated 20 October 1829: 'I'm travelling at 7 o'clock this evening by stagecoach to the Wiesiołowskis near Poznań, which is why I'm writing in advance, especially as I don't know how long I shall be staying there, although I've taken a passport for only a month. My idea is to return in two weeks' time. – One reason for my journey is the presence of Radziwiłł on his estate the other side of Kalisz.'[96]

~ Strzyżew remained in the hands of the Wiesiołowskis from the mid eighteenth century to the 1840s, when it was sold to the Prussian government.

Strzyżew lies in the commune of Sieroszewice, in Ostrów county, in the Greater Poland voivodeship, some 15 km from Antonin.

Antonin

NTONIN LIES IN THE SOUTHERN PART of the Greater Poland voivode-ship. Amidst picturesque woodland, Duke Antoni Radziwiłł, Prussian-appointed governor of the Grand Duchy of Posen, had his estate, named after him. Initially, it served him mainly during the summer months. The duke was a keen hunter, and Antonin was a stately hunting residence, to which society readily travelled from Poznań. There were also frequent visits from personages connected with the Berlin court. With time, as a result of political and personal changes, the governor moved to his Antonin palace for good, together with his wife, Duchess Luiza, the niece of Emperor Ferdinand II, and their two daughters, Wanda and Eliza.

◄ Antonin Palace

~ The Antonin hunting palace was built in the years 1822–24, to a design by the famous Berlin architect Karl Friedrich Schinkel. It is a four-storey timber building, laid out on the plan of a Greek cross: an octagonal main body with three-storey wings, each on a square plan, built onto four of the sides. Its original construction, extremely

▼ Antonin, landscape with palace, 19ᵗʰ c.

▲ Radziwiłł family
burial chapel
at Antonin, designed
by J. H. Haeberlin

modern for those times and both refined and comfortable, also proved to be most ingenious. The palace,
surrounded by an English-style garden, has survived to
the present day without any extensive rebuilding. Erected
nearby was a chapel, in which the members of the
Radziwiłł family were interred.

～ Thanks to the Radziwiłłs, this beautiful estate, situated amidst extensive old
woodland, close to two lakes—the Szperek and the Wydymacz—became a thriving
cultural centre, in which, besides the above-mentioned hunts, the main pursuits
were music, literature and art. The duke's elder daughter, Eliza, excelled in painting
and produced two portraits of Fryderyk during this time, of which the composer
was greatly appreciative.

～ Duke Radziwiłł, an educated man of wide-ranging interests, was on friendly
terms with the leading artists of his day. He was an admirer and patron of the arts,
a cellist and composer. His oeuvre included numerous small-scale instrumental
pieces, many songs and also music composed to the text of Goethe's *Faust*, which
he held in particularly high esteem. As an experienced patron, he was able to spot
the genius of the young Chopin—his exceptional individuality as a composer and
virtuoso. Fryderyk visited Antonin at the duke's invitation in the autumn of 1829.
His stay lasted just over a week,[97] during which time music could be frequently

heard at the palace, as could discussion on musical subjects.

～ Also during his stay, Chopin composed his Polonaise in C major, Op. 3 for piano and cello, doubtless intended to be performed with the duke, who for his part showed Fryderyk the still incomplete score of his music to *Faust*. Besides this, Fryderyk also gladly gave a few lessons to Wanda, the Radziwiłłs' younger daughter. He mentions his stay at Antonin in a letter to Tytus Woyciechowski in Poturzyn: 'I received your last letter, in which you bade me kiss myself, at Radziwiłł's residence in Antonin. I was there for a week, and you'll not believe how well I felt there. I returned by the last mail-coach and barely excused myself from extending my stay. As for my own person and passing amusement, I would have stayed there until I was chased away, but my affairs, and my Concerto in particular, not yet finished, and impatiently awaiting the completion of its finale, compelled me to leave that paradise. There were two Eves there, the duke's young daughters, extremely good and polite, musical, tender creatures.'[98]

～ After describing his impressions of the duke's musical style, Fryderyk proceeded to his traditional sharing with Tytus of a host of other detailed information: 'I wrote there an alla polacca with cello', he wrote of the Polonaise, 'Nothing to it but dazzle, for the salon, for the ladies; I wanted, you see, the duke's daughter Wanda to learn. - Young, 17 years old, pretty, and it was truly a pleasure to place her little fingers on the keys. But joking aside, she has a considerable and genuine feel for music, such that one need not chatter: crescendo here, piano there, now quicker, now slower, and so on.'[99]

~ The larch palace at Antonin, untouched by war, has survived to the present day in almost perfect condition. The building not only looks, but indeed is, the same building in which the young composer stayed. In the opinion of many observers and scholars, it is 'authentic testimony to Chopin's visit'. Unfortunately, only few such objects remain today on the map of Chopin sites in Poland.

~ The interior of the main body of the palace comprises a three-storey Hearth Room (also known as the hunting room), with a column rising through all three storeys, adorned by antlers, which emphasise the palace's hunting character. Hung on the walls are portraits of Antoni Radziwiłł, his daughters, Wanda and Eliza, and Fryderyk Chopin. There is also a grand piano in the room.

~ Since 1978 one of the side rooms has housed a Music Salon, containing such items as publications relating to Antonin, a cast of the composer's hand, his death-mask, a Buchholtz piano, portraits of Chopin and his bust. In one of the wings, by the main entrance to the palace, a staircase leads up to the floors and balconies located on the first and second storeys of the Hearth Room, from which one can see into the rooms of the side wings.

~ The palace stands in extensive grounds, with a moat and monuments of nature, dominated by oaks. The palace grounds and the adjoining wood occupy a total of over twelve hectares.

~ In the years 1974–78 the palace underwent conservation work. Since 1981 it has functioned as a Centre for Creative Work. In 1994 fire consumed part of the roof. In recent years a gas boiler-house has been erected and the main room has been refurnished. The palace offers accommodation for guests, and the Hearth Room houses a restaurant and cafe.

~ In front of the palace stands a bust of Fryderyk Chopin made by Marian Owczar-ski. By the entrance to the building a commemorative plaque has been set into the wall, funded by Igo Moś of Ostrzeszów, with the following inscription: 'Fryderyk Chopin 1810–1849 was a guest at the palace in Antonin in the years 1827 and 1829'. The building is owned by the Kalisz Centre for Culture and the Arts.

~ Many events are held at the palace, including concerts, exhibitions and symposia. Among the traditional events are anniversary concerts (in February and October, on the anniversary of Chopin's birth and death), Shrovetide concerts (in January), the 'Chopin for the Youngest' International Piano Competition (in February), the Tournament of Foreign Piano Scholarship Holders (in April), Chopin Confrontations (in July and August), a cycle of concerts and the All-Poland Chopin Autumn Rally (in September) for tourists on foot, cycle and horseback, ending with a concert.

~ The most important event organised in the Radziwiłłs' ducal hunting palace is the international festival Chopin in the Colours of Autumn (a four-day event in September). For over twenty years now, outstanding performing artists have travelled to the festival from all over the world. The event is very well attended, especially the Saturday-Sunday concert Chopin in the Velvet of the Night. The event is co-organised by the Greater Poland Chopin Centre – Antonin and the Kalisz Centre for Culture and the Arts.

Antonin is situated on the edge of the Barycz Valley Landscape Park, within the commune of Przygodzice, in Ostrów county, in the Greater Poland voivodeship; it is a centre for rest and recreation. The Przygodzice commune is also home to the Wydymacz nature reserve, Przygodzice Lake and a Protected Landscape Area. The village lies 12 km from Ostrów Wielkopolski and 40 km from Kalisz.

Worth seeing in the area:

► forester's lodge and two cottages designed by Karl Friedrich Schinkel (in Swiss style) in Antonin,

► Dębnica—a village to which Chopin went on walks, picturesquely situated in the vicinity of fish ponds, surrounded on three sides by woodland,

► Strzyżew—a village in which the composer stayed at the home of his godmother, Anna Wiesiołowska, née Skarbek.

Poznań

FRYDERYK DECIDED TO DEVOTE THE EARLY AUTUMN of 1828 to his first longer journey abroad. Although he had already crossed the 'Polish border' on several occasions, he had never yet been to Berlin. The Chopins' family friend, Professor Feliks Paweł Jarocki, was travelling to Berlin for a naturalists' congress and invited Fryderyk to accompany him. Thanks to this trip, the young man had the chance to become acquainted with the Berlin music milieu.

⁓ On 9 September 1828 Chopin left with Professor Jarocki by stagecoach for Berlin. The route led through Poznań, where they had only a two-hour break in their journey. According to an hypothesis advanced by Henryk F. Nowaczyk, they used this time to deliver an important package entrusted them by Julian Ursyn Niemcewicz, containing 'documents designed to surmount the bureaucratic obstacles erected by the Prussian authorities over the transferral from Berlin to Gniezno of the mortal remains of Archbishop Ignacy Krasicki'.[100] On reaching Poznań, the two travellers set off in the direction of the Archbishops' Palace, in order to deliver the eagerly awaited parcel in person to Archbishop Teofil Wolicki.[101] It is possible that the archbishop invited his guests to dinner, at the same time encouraging them to spend more time in Poznań on their return journey.

⁓ It is thought that Chopin and Professor Jarocki did indeed spend a few days in Poznań on their way back to Warsaw around the turn of September and October (from 30 September to 3 October 1828). There is no certainty as to their accommodation in the city; could it have been 'the Hotel Saski on ul. Wrocławska, usually frequented by travellers'?[102] Most probably, as previously agreed, they went for dinner to the palace of Archbishop Wolicki.

◄ Poznań Palace
(former Jesuit college)

There is insufficient information in sources to confirm the hypothesis that Chopin performed at the Poznań residence of Duke Antoni Radziwiłł, who, as governor of the Grand Duchy of Posen, lived in the palace on Plac Kolegiacki.

⁓ It might have seemed, and has indeed been accepted in the subject literature, that Henryk Siemiradzki's painting *Koncert Fryderyka Chopina w salonie księcia Antoniego Radziwiłła w 1829 r.* [A concert given by Fryderyk Chopin in the salon of Duke Antoni Radziwiłł in 1829] (which supposedly shows the Radziwiłłs of Antonin and Chopin during a recital) was an iconographic representation of an historical fact. However, this is a false interpretation. Moreover, it is not certain that the Radziwiłłs, or at least the duke himself, were present in Poznań at that time (around the end of September and the beginning of October 1828).[103]

⁓ Fryderyk Chopin's stay in Poznań is commemorated by two plaques and a bust. One of the plaques is situated near the Adam Mickiewicz Monument on the east-

facing wall in the courtyard of the building that houses the Poznań Society for the Friends of Learning, together with its Library and Meeting Hall, and the Poznań Academic Library (at 27/29 ul. Seweryna Mielżyńskiego). The plaque is made

▲ Poznań Town Hall, lithograph by K. F. Dietrich, 1835

of marble and brass and features a medallion with the composer's likeness and an inscription: 'To Chopin, 1810–1849'. The work of Władysław Marcinkowski, the plaque was unveiled in 1910. Destroyed during the Nazi occupation, it was reconstructed after 1945.[104]

~ The other plaque was set into the front wall, near the entrance, of the baroque building that formerly housed the Jesuit college (17 Plac Kolegiacki). Made of dark granite, it proclaims that: 'In 1828 Fryderyk Chopin played in this building'. It was unveiled on 16 October 1960.[105] Behind this building, on ul. Podgórna, is a small park named after Chopin, with a bust of the composer made by Marcin Rożek. This was originally unveiled in 1923 in Stanisław Moniuszko Park in Poznań. It was held in safekeeping during the war and in 1961 placed in its new site, in the Fryderyk Chopin Park. In 1997 the bust was destroyed by a bomb explosion. A copy was produced, which was unveiled in 1999 (in Fryderyk Chopin Park). In that same year the previous bust was unveiled after restoration in the White Room of the Poznań Municipal Offices.[106]

~ The Jesuit college in Poznań was erected in the first half of the eighteenth century (replacing the Renaissance college built towards the end of the sixteenth century). In spite of minor alterations made during the nineteenth century, its monumental baroque structure has survived to the present day. It combines the forms of monastery and palace. The palatial complex also includes the church of St Stanislaus the Martyr (on Plac Kolegiacki at the exit of ul. Gołębia). In 1773 the Jesuit Order was abolished. In 1793, when the city was occupied by the Prussians, the building became home to the Prussian administration. During the period of the Grand Duchy of Warsaw, the building was the headquarters of Prince Friedrich August, Saxon Elector (from 1806 King of Saxony) and Grand Duke of Warsaw. Following the Congress of Vienna, it was inhabited for many years by Duke Antoni Radziwiłł, with his wife, Luiza, née Hohenzollern. The building now houses the Municipal Offices of Poznań.

~ In the Museum of Musical Instruments (at 45 Stary Rynek [Market Square]), in the Chopin Room (first floor, room 9), there stands the piano on which Chopin played during his visit to Duke Antoni Radziwiłł at Antonin. There is also a cast of Chopin's hand and his death-mask, Henryk Siemiradzki's painting *Koncert Fryderyka Chopina w salonie księcia Antoniego Radziwiłła w 1829 r.* [A concert given by Fryderyk Chopin in the salon of Duke Antoni Radziwiłł in 1829] a bust of the composer (in lime, design by Wacław Szymanowski), a portrait of Chopin and an upright piano by 'Traugott Berndt – Breslau' from *c.*1850.

Poznań is one of the oldest and largest cities in Poland, capital of the Greater Poland voivodeship. It lies on the River Vistula, on the E30 and DK11 roads.

Żychlin

P RESERVED TO THIS DAY IN ŻYCHLIN, near Konin, is the Evangelical church and palace which, on 2–4 September 1829, Fryderyk Chopin and his companions on the journey to Vienna, Alfons Brandt and Ignacy Maciejowski, visited in the company of Dr Adam Bogumił Helbich. Held in Żychlin during those days was the wedding of Melania Bronikowska (1811–34) and Wiktor Kurnatowski (1806–47). Preserved in the Evangelical parish records, held in the State Archive in Poznań, is the marriage certificate, from which we learn that the ceremony took place on 2 September 1829 at 12 noon, and that they were married by the Revd Jan Jakub Scholtz.[107]

~ However, in his memoirs published on the pages of the *Tygodnik Ilustrowany*, Adam Helbich writes that they arrived in Żychlin 'towards evening', and so were not present at the wedding. But they did attend the reception, which went on until the third day; the guests left around 2 p.m. Here is an excerpt from Helbich's memoirs:

~ 'It so happened that I was travelling to the Bs' in Z. as an invited guest at the celebrations of their daughter's wedding. Knowing that in a home celebrated for its good, old-fashioned hospitality, three well-educated young men would be well received, I invited them to accompany me.

They willingly agreed.

And so we set off. Towards evening we arrive at the palace. The host, in merry mood, greets us with open arms, and numerous guests look out from all the windows. A moment later we all felt at home, as if among our very own relatives. Among the guests was Mr Henryk U., who greeted my companions like good acquaintances. He had met them in Reinertz, and before a quarter of an hour had passed all those present had already learned of Fryderyk's noble deed [concert for orphans in Duszniki].

◄ Interior of the Evangelical church in Żychlin

I shall not dwell here over a description of the amusements of that solemn day. I'll just say that the time flew by like a shot, under the effect of the music, dancing and animation of the whole company.

On the third day the time came to depart. The young guests were anxious to return to their families in Warsaw. From 11 in the morning the horses stood harnessed, but has it ever occurred that someone has left the home of their host without breakfast? So the horses had to wait. 12 o'clock struck and the guests assembled in the hall. In the adjoining dining-room, lively conversations were taking place while the company waited for the table to be laid.

▲ Żychlin Palace

Then someone made a proposal:
– To round off the amusements, let's play some society games, and since we are to go off in various directions, let's play traveller.
– And so the names of cities were given out and everyone took care to be ready; in spite of this, however, there was no lack of forfeits.
– When the turn came for Mr Henryk to pay a forfeit, one of the ladies gave him a task to do which would have been to the liking of all those present.
– He thought for a while and then ran out. A moment later, he came back, carrying an ivy branch tied in a ribbon, and placing it on Fryderyk's head he said:
– I crown talent and virtue.
There followed a long and thunderous ovation, continuously renewed. Tears ran down Fryderyk's cheeks, and there seemed not a dry eye among all those assembled.'[108]
∼ The composer himself gave an account of his stay in Żychlin in a letter to Tytus Woyciechowski dated 12 September 1829: 'And I, on the way back, was at the wedding reception of Miss Melania Bronikowska: a lovely child, wed Kurnatowski'.[109]
∼ It is worth mentioning that there were two pairs of newlyweds at the reception, the other couple being Aniela Kurnatowska[110] and Wojciech Gałczyński, whose marriage had taken place a few days earlier, on 25 August 1829 in the Roman Catholic church in the village of Charłupia, near Sieradz.

~ The church in Żychlin was built in the years 1821–22 in place of the previous old timber church. It is a building in classicist style, on a rectangular plan. The church's interior is simple and ascetic, with a centrally placed pulpit and Lord's table, bearing the following inscription: 'Blessed are the pure at heart'. On either side are two epitaphs: to Melania Kurnatowska and Teodor Pretwic, whilst the side walls are adorned with two portraits of great benefactors of the parish: Joanna Florentyna Bronikowska, née Potworowska, and her husband, Adam Bronikowski. A plaque devoted to the memory of Melania Kurnatowska, placed below a tin urn, reads as follows: 'Here Wiktor Kurnatowski preserved the heart of his wife, Melania Kurnatowska, née Bronikowska, RIP, b. 16 July 1811, d. 31 Oct. 1834.'

~ Almost exactly opposite the church stands a palace. This is thought to have been built in the early 1820s. Before this there was a timber manor house in Żychlin.[111] There is no information as to the appearance of the new walled building. It is presumed to have been similar to the present edifice. However, it certainly looked different inside. Żychlin Palace was built on a rectangular plan, with a front porch covered by a hip-roof. It stands in grounds covering 2.5 hectares, in which monuments of nature have survived: ashes, lindens and a plane. Today, the building is the seat of a School of Economics and Services.

~ In order to commemorate the composer's stay in Żychlin, on 2 September 1999 a bronze plaque was set into the front wall of the palace, by the main entrance. The idea of Henryk Janasek, it was made by Giotto Dimitrow. Its inscription reads as follows: 'Here, in the first days of September 1829, stayed Fryderyk Chopin'.

Żychlin lies a few kilometres from Konin, in Konin county, in the Greater Poland voivodeship.

Worth seeing in the area:
- ▶ fifteenth-century gothic church of St Bartholomew (with late Renaissance chapel) in Konin,
- ▶ gothic church from the first half of the fifteenth century in Gosławice,
- ▶ classicist presbytery from 1839 attached to the church in Żychlin,
- ▶ bell-tower founded in 1788 by Adam Feliks Bronikowski (moved in 1821 to a stone base) in Żychlin
- ▶ mausoleum from 1840 in Żychlin.

Sulechów

I N BIOGRAPHICAL STUDIES, from Maurycy Karasowski onwards, the halt at the 'post office in Sulechów' on the route from Berlin to Poznań with Professor Feliks Jarocki is traditionally named as the venue of an improvised performance by Fryderyk: 'On arriving at the village of Zullichów (Zullichau), they were told at the post depot that the lack of horses meant they would have to wait for about an hour. So Professor Jarocki suggested to his young companion that they take a walk around the village; on returning from their walk, and seeing that the stagecoach was still not ready, they entered the house which served as post office and restaurant in one. Fryderyk immediately espied in the adjoining room, a sort of drawing-room, a piano; he walks up to it, opens it, and gives it a try: "Ah! Out of tune" he says with a kind of satisfaction, sits down and starts to play.'[112]

~ The fact that this episode is not confirmed in sources already drew doubts from Ferdynand Hoesick, but only intense research over the last decade of the twentieth century brought more information on this subject. A clear opponent of the idea that Chopin stopped in Sulechów is Henryk F. Nowaczyk, who maintains that the story is merely a legend with many different versions. An analysis of the stagecoach timetable and postal routes, as well as the checking of many other elements to the story, led this scholar to conclude that the description of the Sulechów episode possessed only 'a tiny grain of truth'.

~ The inhabitants have commemorated Chopin's hypothetical stay in Sulechów[113] with a plaque bearing the composer's likeness, set into the wall of the town hall's tower (at 6 Plac Ratuszowy), which displays the dates of Chopin's birth and death and a quotation from Cyprian Kamil Norwid's poem 'Fortepian Chopina' [Chopin's piano]: 'And there was in this Poland, from the zenith / of the omniperfection of history / taken, with a rainbow of wonder:/ Poland—of wheelwrights[114] transformed!' Below this is the inscription: 'In commemoration of the 130th anniversary of Fryderyk Chopin's stay in Sulechów in September 1828. The inhabitants of Sulechów 1958.'

~ The town hall building has known numerous changes over the centuries. Preserved to the present day are parts of the walls and the cellar vaults from the times of its construction. The town hall was radically rebuilt in the second half of the nineteenth century, when a third storey was added. The building now houses the Municipal Offices, the Registry Office and the Town Council.

~ Sulechów is also home to the Fryderyk Chopin Centre for Culture and Sport (at 3 Aleja Wielkopolska) and the Fryderyk Chopin Cultural Society.

Sulechów lies about 20 km north-east of Zielona Góra in the Lubusz Uplands, in the northern part of Zielona Góra county, in the Lubusz voivodeship.
The southern part of the Sulechów commune is traversed by the River Oder and its tributaries the Sulechówka and Rakówka. The commune features a quite large area of woodland (approx. 40%), monuments of nature and quite high hills.

Worth seeing in the area:

▶ Church of the Blessed Virgin Mary (from the fourteenth century, with gothic-Renaissance interior) in Klępsk,

▶ late gothic church, palace and chapel in Kalsk,

▶ 'Krosno' town gate, the only one of four gates dating from 1704 to have survived, in Sulechów,

▶ fragments of the town wall from the beginning of the fourteenth century in Sulechów,

▶ late gothic parish church of the Elevation of the Holy Cross in Sulechów.

VI

Lesser Poland (Małopolska)

Cracow

'We spent the first week in Cracow
just walking around and visiting the surrounding area'[115]

AFTER AN EXCEPTIONALLY HARDWORKING academic year, summed
up by Elsner in his school report with the famous opinion 'Szopen Friderik
– Special ability, musical genius',[116] in the second half of July 1829 Fryderyk
set off with a few friends on a journey abroad to Vienna.

~ The route of this journey led through Cracow, where the party had planned a
lengthy stay to visit the city and the area around it. This was Chopin's only visit
to Cracow, and letters to his parents and to Tytus Woyciechowski show that he

► Church of St Mary in Cracow,
lithograph by K. F. Dietrich,
1835

◄ Church of St Mary
in Cracow

(175)

▲ Cloth Hall [Sukiennice] on the Market Square in Cracow

remembered it as a cheerful and fruitful holiday jaunt. Among the party were Fryderyk's friends Alfons Brandt and Mieczysław Potocki, as well as the Latinist Marceli Celiński. The senior member of the expedition (albeit barely six years older than Fryderyk) was Romuald Hube, a lecturer on the law department of Warsaw University. It was he who took upon himself the responsibility for the journey.

~ Here is an extract from his memoirs: 'wishing as far as possible to discharge the duties entrusted in me, and becoming increasingly certain of what a great deal I lack, for the more one learns, the more one becomes convinced of one's ineptitude, every holiday I travelled abroad, and that with the aim of acquiring some knowledge and of learning what I lacked [...] When in 1828 I was leaving for Vienna, placed in my care to be accompanied to Vienna was the young Chopin, already distinguishing himself with the extraordinary talent which later would so dazzle the musical world.'[117]

~ Hube, greatly liked and esteemed by Chopin, was the guide during the journey—something which doubtless increased its appeal. He possessed excellent knowledge of the cities in which they stopped. He had lived in Cracow with his family for several years and attended St Anne's gymnasium school there.

~ Unfortunately, it is difficult to establish today where Chopin stayed during those few days spent in Cracow. The only wholly secure information concerning his sojourn is the fact that he visited the most magnificent of the city's gothic buildings,

▲ View over the Market Square and Town Hall in Cracow, lithograph by K. F. Dietrich, 1820

namely Collegium Maius—the original seat of the Jagiellonian Academy (University). We know that he perused the valuable collections held at the college, which in Chopin's day housed the Jagiellonian Library, at the junction of ul. św. Anny and ul. Jagiellońska. This is attested by the composer's signature in the visitors' book under the date 23 July 1829. The manuscript (shelf-mark 1794, fo. 86), which is held in the Jagiellonian Library, also carries the entries made by the friends who travelled with him.

~ A better idea of how a visit to the Jagiellonian Academy of Cracow might have looked in those times can be gained from the memoirs of the Chopins' friend Klementyna Hoffmanowa, née Tańska, who made a longer journey to Cracow two years before Fryderyk. Here is an extract from her notes for 30 May 1827:[118] 'Alongside the most agreeable and social pleasures which the inexpressibly kind inhabitants of Cracow lavish upon us, barely during those two days did we find the time to take a good look around Cracow Academy, its library, classrooms and church. – The Jagiellonian Academy has about it the gravity of years, the charm of recollections and the stamp of antiquity; and although it does not set before our eyes those great edifices to which modern architecture has accustomed us, it speaks to the mind and the heart. It is cramped on a rather narrow street, St Anne's, and reminds us in this of the times when it was built.'

Mogiła Kościuszki   Le Tertre de Kościuszko

~ Perhaps surprisingly, the forms applied in the architecture of Collegium Maius, rooted mainly in the Polish and German gothic, do not give it a gloomy character. 'The academy's courtyard is not very large, but it seems unchanged since it was laid out; those galleries have an utterly ancient aspect – not with magnificence, but with age do they arouse our respect...'[119] This magical building exudes an air of humanism. It is worth mentioning that the gothic university buildings are among the most exceptional in the world.[120] Crucially, when the Jagiellonian University was visited by Chopin (and by Klementyna Tańska shortly before him), Collegium Maius still retained its original, gothic character. Later, in the 1860s, its was rebuilt in a neo-gothic style, which for many years disfigured the building. Tańska's description may be compared with its present-day appearance, as post-war reconstruction, completed in the 1960s, restored the building to its old form, revealing the virtues of the noble gothic.

▲ Kościuszko Mound, lithograph by J. Sonntag, first half of 19th c.

~ The continuation of Tańska's description is also worth quoting extensively: 'One may gain some idea of the history of the Academy in the Jagiellonian Hall. This is a building that is most fascinating, and even beautiful; it has ancient monuments, such as the grand gothic windows with little panes and a ceiling in squares, from the middle of which gold roses of different shapes grow out; for centuries this has been the venue for councils, meetings and all academic ceremonies; in recent times this hall fell into almost complete ruin, but the efforts of the keen citizen, Revd Sebastian Sierakowski, have restored the integrity of this work of Kings, this dear souvenir of centuries past; and under his enlightened direction, the brush of Sta-chowicz has represented the Academy's history in eleven tableaux painted on the wall.[121] [...] From this hall, which is further adorned by emblems of all the sciences and arts, symbolically represented, various inscriptions, likenesses of illustrious pupils, first of all, then masters of this Academy, we passed to its Library.[122] [...] The Library was established from donations; the oldest of those preserved to the present day is a donation by Jan, son of Andrzej of Nissa, Letters of St Paul copied out in the year 1666, and thus was it continually enhanced, for the monetary funds were always so meagre that it could purchase nothing.'[123] Indeed, as Tańska stresses, the library was enriched chiefly thanks to donations from affluent and worldly Poles, most often from the wealthy families of students and also, traditionally, pro-fessors of the Academy. Unfortunately, the famous collection never benefited from the permanent patronage of the Polish court: 'For a long time, up to the begin-ning of the 16th century, there was no common book collection, each department of learning having its own separate collection of books and manuscripts, not until 4 March 1517 did Tomasz Obiedziński put forward the idea of fitting out two rooms as a common library [...] the two rooms constitute the main body of the library to the present day, and bear Obiedziński's name.'[124]

~ A period of prosperity, when the library collections were continually expanded, thanks to access to books printed in the presses being founded at that time in Cracow, were followed by leaner years. These followed the death of King Stephen Báthory, when the entire Academy fell into considerable decline; a succession of historic events and wartime looting brought almost total collapse upon the library. In the years 1699–1774 the collections were deposited in sealed chests. Under the initiative of Revd Putanowicz, work began on returning the library to academic use, and these labours continued over the next few generations.

~ From 1811 the librarian was Jerzy Samuel Bandtkie, who succeeded in consider ably improving the state of all the library rooms, as well as the collection itself and its catalogues. It was Bandtkie who was Klementyna Tańska's guide in 1827, and the quoted extracts from her descriptions were certainly inspired by infor-mation passed on by him. It is possible that similar stories were heard two years later by the friends visiting Collegium Maius; perhaps they were also shown around the library by Jerzy Samuel Bandtkie...

~ Klementyna Tańska relates that the library collection in those times numbered '2,100 manuscripts of over 35,000 works, up to 20,000 treatises and booklets. Among the manuscripts it has works by the classic writers of antiquity, and among the prints many incunabula, that is, works which were the first to be printed, fol-lowing the invention of that inestimable art; it has atlases and a not inconsiderable collection of geographical maps, especially depicting Poland.'[125]

⌁ Tańska also enumerates several titles of manuscripts which she was able to examine more closely in the library. These in-

▲ Courtyard of Collegium Maius in Cracow

clude Pliny's Natural History and letters to Vespasian, collections of sermons by Mikołaj Wiganda and Paweł of Zator from the early fifteenth century, and Kacper Niesiecki's *Herbarz* [Armorial], with handwritten footnotes by Ignacy Krasicki.

⌁ In further descriptions, Tańska mentions: 'A quarter part of the records of Princes and more excellent persons'. From 1775, the library became essentially a sort of 'library-museum', and these records were made into a visitors' book; 'I saw the names of Kościuszko, the King of Saxony, Prince Józef Poniatowski',[126] writes Tańska. Thanks to this fitting tradition, today we have a document confirming that Chopin visited the Jagiellonian Library. We also know the exact date of this visit and the names of his companions there.

⌁ Fryderyk's attention is certain to have been drawn to all the above-mentioned books of particular value by Romuald Hube, who, as we learn from his Memoirs, was a connoisseur of old books. On his numerous journeys around Europe, Hube most diligently visited all the libraries along his route. Whenever he could, he would spend all his free time there, perusing not only law-related literature, but also collections devoted to art.

◀ Collegium Maius, *Wniyście do Sali Jagielloṅskiey* [Entrance to the Jagiellonian Hall], M. Stachowicz, first quarter of 19th c.

∼ In recalling her visit to Collegium Maius, Taṅska goes on to mention the classrooms for physics, chemistry and mineralogy which she was shown around by professors.

∼ A great variety of interesting objects were assembled in the museum collection at that time. Besides numerous works of art, valuable paintings and sculptures, including a collection of portraits of professors, there were also archaeological exhibits, historical items, scientific instruments, a numismatic collection, and also a collection of 'rarities', continually enriched since the sixteenth century. The most valuable items were gathered in the university treasury, in a collection founded by Queen Jadwiga.

∼ Sources document the fact that Fryderyk passed along ul. Św. Anna. So he is certain to have been many a time on the Market Square and the nearby parts of the city, admiring the Cloth Hall, St Mary's Church, St Florian's Gate and the Barbican.

~ One may assume that Fryderyk also visited Wawel Hill during his stay. In spite of the fact that in the first half of the nineteenth century the neglected hill was not a generally accessible tourist attraction, the young men, eager for historical knowledge, would certainly not have omitted to make a lengthy visit to the castle and the magnificent cathedral. There is no question that Chopin could have failed to take in that most important of Polish centres for liturgical music, celebrated for its centuries-old tradition.

~ By contrast to the castle, which was but a shadow of its former glory, in Wawel Cathedral Fryderyk had the opportunity of admiring the greatest of treasures, masterpieces of architecture, sculpture and painting. It is possible that music could be heard in this extraordinary interior. As Mieczysław Tomaszewski supposes, Fryderyk may have listened to the sound of the organ, played by the outstanding virtuoso Wincenty Gorączkiewicz.[127]

~ It is no easy task to describe succinctly the history of Wawel Hill, as it reaches back to the dawn of the Polish state. The construction of the present Wawel Cathedral was commenced in the beginning of the eleventh century, on the site of the two previous churches. It was founded by Bishop Nanker and King Ladislaus I the Elbow-high. From those times on, the cathedral was associated with the coronation and funeral ceremonies of virtually all Polish rulers. Mixed together in its brick-stone walls are several styles of architecture. It is a three-aisled basilica with three towers (the sixteenth-century Sigismund's Tower [Wieża Zygmuntowska] is topped by a famous bell, until recently the biggest in Poland). The eighteen chapels around the cathedral include an impressive array of masterpieces, including Sigismund's Chapel [Kaplica Zygmuntowska], a gem of Renaissance architecture in Italian style. Among the basilica's treasures are a seventeenth-century silver sarcophagus with relics of St Stanislaus the Martyr, a main altar with an image of Christ Crucified, where rulers were crowned, the gothic crucifix of Queen Jadwiga (the work of Veit Stoss), richly decorated baroque choir stalls, and also an extraordinary group of royal tombstones, adorned with the effigies of the deceased rulers. The cathedral crypts contain the graves of members of royal families and many eminent Poles.

~ From the mid eleventh century, Wawel Castle became the royal seat. The most significant rebuilding of the castle, in the then obligatory Renaissance style, was carried out in the sixteenth century, during the reigns of Aleksander Jagiellończyk and Sigismund I the Old. We know the names of four of the masters who made a great contribution to the construction of this splendid edifice: Eberhard Rosemberger, Franciszek Florentczyk, Bartolomeo Berrecci and Benedykt of Sandomierz. Also applied at that time was the symbolic decoration of the building's exterior, partly modified in baroque style around the turn of the sixteenth and seventeenth centuries.

~ Unfortunately, from the beginning of the seventeenth century, when the last king to reside in Cracow, Sigismund III, left Wawel Hill, the state of the buildings gradually deteriorated. In the eighteenth century, this exceptional Renaissance monument began to decline considerably, and after the Third Partition of Poland, the Austrian army set up barracks on the site. And it was during this period, perhaps the worst in the castle's history, that it befell Chopin to visit the old royal castle.

~ A whole week of intense walking and visiting the Cracow area made a powerful impression on Fryderyk. He wrote about this exciting expedition in a letter to his friend, Tytus Woyciechowski: 'In merry company, albeit a little foreign, I travelled to Vienna, and if Cracow engrossed me such that I devoted but little time to thinking about home and about you, then Vienna so intoxicated, enchanted and beguiled me that I went two weeks without any letters from home and felt no yearning.'[128]

~ The entry made by Chopin in the visitors' book in 1829 is held in the Manuscripts Section of the Jagiellonian Library. At the time the composer was in Cracow, the Jagiellonian Library was housed in Collegium Maius, which is now home to the Jagiellonian University Museum (at 15 ul. Jagiellońska, on the corner with ul. św. Anny). The present shape of this building is linked to a rebuilding in Romantic style that was carried out over several stages during the nineteenth century. Retained, however, was the gothic structure of the quadrangular building with gallery-lined courtyard. Marvellously preserved are the interiors, in which one may admire a display of items documenting the history of the Academy/University in Cracow.

~ Numerous Chopin souvenirs have been gathered in Cracow,[129] including manuscripts, autographs of his compositions and letters, portraits and busts[130]. One of the most important exhibits is the Pleyel piano on which the composer played during his sojourn in Scotland in 1848. This stands in the Green Room [Sala Zielona] of Collegium Maius. Chopin wrote an autograph inside the case: 'Frederic Chopin, 15 novembre 1848'. For some time the piano was the property of Chopin's pupil and admirer, Jane W. Stirling (1804–59), who was already collecting items connected with him while her master was still alive. The instrument then passed into the hands of her heir, her niece's daughter, and then the music critic Edouard Ganche (1880–1945) of Lyons. It ended up in its present location from the Ganche collection.

ANSTALT

für Salz-Soole-Salzdampf – Salzschlamm
Douche – und Tropf- Bäder, auch mit Schwe-
felquelle, Schwefelleber und Malzabsad, in

WIELICZKA

durch eine Action-Gesellschaft im Jahre 837,
gegründet und am 15.ten Juni 838 im gröss-
ten Theil eröfnet

Zakład

kąpieli z wodą słoną, z słoney parę, z mułem słonym,
z wodą narełaną, z wątrobą siarki z odwarem słodu;
narszcie rozmaitych spadowych i kroplanych, w

Wieliczce

przez towarzystwo akcyonaruszów w roku 837.
przedsięwzięty, i dnia 15.° Czerwca 1838 w
większey części otworzony;

... a vastness like another town,
and almost a thousand people
buried so many cubits deep in the earth
mine treasures that are veritably
more needed and beneficial than gold...[131]

Wieliczka

INCLUDED IN THE PROGRAMME OF EXCURSIONS around the Cracow area, the group of young men led by Romuald Hube also had a trip to the then fashionable Wieliczka.

~ Now seven hundred years old, this salt mine was opened up as a tourist attraction during the last quarter of the eighteenth century. Around this time, attention began to be drawn to the salt water's healthful properties, and the mine began to offer treatment as a sanatorium. Among the sources of information as to what a visit around Wieliczka looked like during the first half of the nineteenth century are the descriptions of Klementyna Tańska.

~ So it is worth turning once again to her memoirs, as we may, with a good deal of probability, presume that the situations and emotions experienced by Klementyna Tańska during her stay there were similar to those of the young Chopin: 'In pleasant company, comprising five people, having received from the mine's management permission and a guide and declaring that we wished to descend by cable rather than walking down the steps, we proceeded to the mouth of the mine—a place which looks like a shed; in the middle is an opening in the shape of a huge well, and through this the workers and the curious descend; on glancing into these dark depths, through which one is to pass, one senses an involuntary shiver; the quill that one is handed for writing one's name in the book prepared for this purpose shakes slightly in the hand, and the long linen shirt in which the traveller is covered to spare her dress seems to resemble a final deathly garment.'[132]

◄ Salt water spa in Wieliczka,
lithograph, 19th c.

~ Klementyna Tańska goes on to write that anxiety is overcome by curiosity, and that the visitor embarks on a mysterious voyage, in order to examine this remarkable underground town. It should be assumed that Fryderyk went down under the ground to visit the mine; otherwise, he would not have been invited to make an entry (on 23 July 1829) into the visitors' book.

~ Today, the places near Cracow which were visited by Chopin—Wieliczka, Ojców and Pieskowa Skała—are visited by a great many tourists, due to their exceptional attractiveness and their historical and natural significance. Particularly noteworthy among them is the salt mine at Wieliczka (situated at 10 ul. Daniłowicza). In 1978 the mine was inscribed on UNESCO's World Heritage List.

~ Marked out at a depth of 135 metres below ground are tourist trails, along which one can visit the chambers with their collection of mining machines and equipment, the saltwater lakes and the chapel with salt sculptures and bas-reliefs. Most

impressive of all is the Chapel of St Kinga. The mine also runs an underground sanatorium for those with breathing ailments. Beneath the

▲ Wieliczka, steel engraving by K. Rybička, after Fischer, 1843

earth, one may also visit the Cracow Salt Mines' Museum, where the exhibits include salt crystals, the oldest salt-works in Europe, sacred art relics and a panorama of old Wieliczka. Also on display in the museum are reproductions of pages from the visitors' book with the signatures of illustrious guests. These include the signature of Fryderyk Chopin.

Wieliczka is located about 15 km from Cracow, in Wieliczka county, in the Lesser Poland voivodeship. One can travel to Wieliczka from Cracow by road (E40 in the direction of Bochnia); numerous minibuses depart from the Dworzec Główny railway station.

Ojców

T HE GROUP OF FRIENDS made several excursions from Cracow to the surrounding area, including to Prądnik Valley, famed for its magnificent views.

~ Chopin gave a detailed and witty account of the adventure connected with his trip to Ojców (on 26 July 1829) in a letter written to his parents after his arrival in Vienna, on 1 August 1829, edited by Maurycy Karasowski in *Młodość Fryderyka Chopina*:[133]
'Before I begin to describe Vienna, I shall tell you what happened with Ojców. After dinner on Sunday, on hiring a four-horsed Cracow cart for 4 thalers, we paraded around in it as elegantly as you like. Having left behind the city and the beautiful outskirts of Cracow, we had our coachman drive straight to Ojców, believing that to be where Mr Indyk lived—the peasant who usually accommodates all travellers and where Miss Tańska also stayed. To our misfortune, it turned out that Mr Indyk lives a mile from Ojców, and our coachman, not familiar with the road, drove into Prądnik river, actually a crystal-clear stream, and no other road could be found, with rocks to the right and to the left. Around nine in the evening, we were met in this nomadic and clueless state by a couple of people who, taking pity on us, undertook to guide us to Mr Indyk.

▲ Prądnik Valley

▲ View of Ojców with castle,
colour lithograph
by K. F. Dietrich, 19th c.

We had to proceed on foot for a good half a mile, across the dew, amidst a host of rocks and sharp stones. We often had to cross the little river along round logs, and all of this in the dark of night. Eventually, after much toiling, nudging and grumbling, we found the way to Mr Indyk. He was not expecting such tardy guests. He gave us a room beneath the rock, in a cottage purposely built for guests. Izabella!… There where Mrs Tańska stood! So each of my colleagues undresses and dries himself in front of a fire kindled in the hearth by the good Mrs Indyk. I just sit down in a corner, and wet up to the knees I ponder whether to undress and dry myself or not; until I see Mrs Indyk approaching a nearby chamber for bedding; touched by some salutary spirit, I follow her and espy on the table a host of woollen Cracow hats. These hats are double, like a dressing-gown. In desperation I buy one for a zloty, tear it into two, doff by shoes, wrap up my feet, and tying them up well, I thus deliver myself from a certain cold. Approaching the fireplace I drank some wine, laughed with my good colleagues, and in the meantime Mrs Indyk has made up our beds on the floor, where we slept marvellously well.

～ The next part of the account, as related by Karasowski, includes the following passage: 'Fryderyk goes on to describe Ojców, Pieskowa Skała, the Black and King's grottos and the surrounding area in exalted tones, speaking with delight "that be it for nothing other than the true beauty of Ojców it was worth getting soaked". Besides this, the letter', writes Karasowski, 'is filled with a description of Viennese picture galleries which he hastily visited and other details less apt to interest the readers'.

~ In his description of Ojców, including in letters to Tytus and Izabela, Fryderyk refers to the account of Klementyna Tańska, with which he was familiar. Tańska wrote that Prądnik Valley appears in all its glory at Ojców from the mount on which the castle is built. In the mid nineteenth century, the castle was already very neglected, partially ruined, and could not be visited in full: 'only when standing at the foot of the tower, on a pile of rubble, did I see the beauty of Ojców, for that is not in the castle, but in the valley one sees from it; [...] a vast city, built out of bedrock; for here, not on one side of the huge ravine do the rocks extend, but on both sides they jut up in the form of weird and wonderful homes; one cannot even see as far as the end of this city of a Titan's sons and the peaks of the rocks, covered in lofty firs, reach up to the sky. The entire village of Ojców, the further buildings and gardens, and that Prądnik more beautiful still, seem to be a settlement of little creatures—little but beloved of some mighty deity, who on account of their frailty gave them such a fortified shelter. I could not get enough of that view.'[134]

~ In Ojców, concealed among the extraordinary rocks are numerous grottos, many of them visited even today, and interest is enhanced by the stories and legends associated with them. Chopin visited Dark Grotto and Elbow-high's Grotto[135]: 'when that king was forced to flee from Wenceslas of Bohemia, he sought poor shelter in its [the castle's] ruined walls and the caves and caverns of these rocks. Remembering his father's wanderings, his worthy son, Casimir the Great, who on taking to the Polish throne provided our country with so many castles and had the one here built up again, stayed here occasionally, and called it first Ojciec u skały [Father at the rock] and then Ojców [of the Fathers].'

~ Chopin was certainly familiar with the legends connected with Ojców and, as the composer's biographers state, not only from Tańska's accounts.[136]

~ Among Ojcow's attractions is the Castle Mount, with the preserved ruins of its gothic castle, erected in the thirteenth century. The historical house Pod Łokietkiem [Elbow-high's], meanwhile, is home to the Ojców National Park Museum—a history and nature museum named after Professor Władysław Szafer, who brought about the creation of the Ojców National Park.

~ Ojców National Park was founded in 1956, as the sixth national park in Poland. The picturesque landscape of Prądnik Valley consists of white calcareous rocks of extraordinary dimensions and shapes (including Hercules' Club and Diotima's Needle) and also broadleaved (mainly beech) forests. There are almost four hundred caves or grottos within the park, with Elbow-high's Grotto and Dark Grotto among the best known. Characteristic of this area is the presence of numerous species of bird, insect and bat (seventeen varieties), which have become symbols of the park. Visiting the park is facilitated by footpaths, cycle paths and bridal paths.

Pieskowa Skała [Pieskowa Rock]

FOLLOWING THE ADVENTURE IN OJCÓW, the next port of call on the planned route of the group's excursion from Cracow was Pieskowa Skała. ∼ The description by Klementyna Tańska contains the following passage:[137] 'I was ruing the views left behind and keenly desirous of those newly presenting themselves; [...] in this situation, at a yet larger turn in the valley, I saw suddenly and wholly unexpectedly the entire Pieskowa rock, and I forgot about everything. A range of new rocks, higher and stranger still, a mountain high and extensive, on it a magnificent castle, on the other side a beech forest, the freshest verdure, in the middle the Prądnik, here much broader, swollen by a lake, a well-shaped bridge, a cross with the effigy of the Saviour on the rock, and nearest the eye, the famous Hercules' club, or as Wężyk calls it, the club of Krakus, who

> Offering to the Gods the tool of ingenious craftsmanship,
> Fixed here his club, which grew into the ground.

This whole view, as if conjured up by a magic wand, captivated me truly.'
∼ The authoress of these memoirs did not omit to make a thorough tour of the castle. She deemed it one of the best preserved monuments in Poland: 'The Castle of Pieskowa rock must have been once an excellent fortress, as it encloses within it every convenience, a mill, forge, enormous stores: the well struck in the bedrock is so deep that the strongest of men had to

◄ Hercules' Club
at Pieskowa Skała

▼ Pieskowa Skała, colour lithograph
by K. F. Dietrich, 19th c.

pull a full pail from it for eleven minutes; [...] there are even two fruit gardens, to which one walks up forty or so steps and over a roof, for like Semiramide's gardens, they are as if airborne. An exquisite view from virtually all the more important rooms over Prądnik Valley, over the rock and over that club of Hercules or Krakus, which, much broader at the top than at the bottom, appears to stand there by some miracle, guards this castle, and diverts from it the ruinous hand of time.'[138]

~ Pieskowa Skała is located in an exceptionally picturesque area near Cracow, in the southern part of the Cracow-Częstochowa Upland. The gothic castle was built most probably in the mid fourteenth century, and its founder was Casimir the Great. In the sixteenth century an irregular Renaissance edifice with galleries, courtyard and viewing loggia was built on the rock. The castle owes its current form in great measure to a thorough rebuilding and expansion carried out in the second half of the sixteenth century by Stanisław Szafraniec, Voivode of Sandomierz. The result was a splendid Renaissance residence. In the first half of the seventeenth century, the new owner, Michał Zebrzydowski, Voivode of Cracow, carried out further expansion, erecting the castle chapel and modern fortifications enclosing a grand outer courtyard. Around 1656 Pieskowa Skała came into the possession of Jan Wielopolski. In 1718 the castle was destroyed by fire, and was subsequently rebuilt in the first half of the eighteenth century, partly modified in the spirit of the late Baroque.

▶ Pieskowa Skała Castle

~ Under the ownership of the Wielopolskis, Pieskowa Skała was a hunting residence (the hunts organised there were among the most famous in Poland). In the years 1842–96 the castle belonged to the Mieroszewskis. During this period the residence was twice destroyed. As a result of a fire in 1850 the oldest part of the castle collapsed, and in 1863, during the January Rising, the castle was severely damaged by Russian artillery fire. In the years 1902–39 a boarding home was housed in the castle chambers. After World War Two the building was taken over by the State Treasury. In the years 1950–68 it underwent thorough conservation work, which restored the courtyard and loggia to their Renaissance appearance. The castle museum was opened in 1970. It is a branch of the Royal Castle [Zamek Królewski] on Wawel Hill (all the objects on display belong to the Wawel collections).

~ The castle, perched on a hill, is reached by an avenue with steps. Nearby rises an extraordinary calcareous rock, two hundred metres high—Hercules' Club. Next to this are Wernyhora's Rocks.

Ojców and Pieskowa Skała are situated about 30 km from Cracow. They can be reached from Cracow by road (E40 in the direction of Olkusz).

VII

Chelmland
(Ziemia Chełmska)

Chelmland

CHOPIN'S JOURNEY TO CHELMLAND was closely linked to his great friendship with Tytus Woyciechowski, who hailed from Poturzyn.

~ Tytus, two years Fryderyk's senior, attended the Warsaw Lyceum and boarded with the Chopins. For the young Chopin, he was a very special figure, in whom he placed enormous trust. From Chopin's reminiscences, one infers that he spent with his older friend long hours in countless discussions, amusements and walks around 'the whole city'; the two friends' favourite route led 'from Nowy Świat up to Sigismund's Column'.

~ On completing his schooling at the Lyceum, Tytus studied on the law department of Warsaw University. Before long, due to his father's premature death, he was forced to take over the duties connected with possession of an extensive estate in Chelmland and moved to the family home in Poturzyn. Tytus's departure, in July 1828, gave rise to an intense exchange of letters between the two young men. Chopin wrote to Tytus very often, relating to him current events and anecdotes, and also confiding in him the secrets of his soul, his musical dilemmas and all his disparate moods. Due to the considerable distance that separated them, this was the only form of 'conversation' open to Chopin with his friend, whom he sorely missed in Warsaw: 'Come for just a breather from your country labours to the bosom of friendship, Miss Sonntag will sing to you and you'll gain new strength for your occupations. What a shame that, instead of a letter, I cannot send myself',[139] rued Fryderyk in a letter to Tytus of 5 June 1830, since on that day only post was being taken from Warsaw 'in the direction of Hrubieszów', and he had to wait for the stagecoach several days more.

◄ Manor grounds
in Poturzyn

Poturzyn

IN THE SUMMER OF 1830 Fryderyk set off on the '40-mile route' to 'the State of Poturzyn'. Many hypotheses appear in biographical studies concerning the route 'in the direction of Hrubieszów'. Most of these suggest that the choice fell on the 'old historical route along the Vistula', through Piaseczno, Czersk, Góra, Ryczywół, Kozienice, Puławy, Końskowola, Lublin, Krasnystaw, Zamość and Komarów to Oszczów.[140] It seems highly probable that the route commenced on 12 July by stagecoach led through Krasnystaw, where there was a transfer to the 'extra-post' travelling through Hrubieszów to Poturzyn.

▲ Remains of the sugar factory once erected by Tytus Woyciechowski

〜The Woyciechowskis possessed an expansive flatland estate, including Poturzyn (also enumerated in the source literature are Żabcze and Witków). In a splendid park with a small lake stood a manor house with hothouses, and with numerous farm buildings in the vicinity. This was certainly a very successful holiday, lasting around a week, later remembered as the 'Poturzyn adventures'—a relaxing sojourn in beautiful surroundings in the company of his best friend, with music everpresent. During this period, Fryderyk valued particularly highly Tytus's honest opinion with regard to his compositions, as he confessed in a letter dated 27 March 1830: 'Your single view after each concert would be worth to me more than all the praise of the critics, Elsners, Kurpińskis, Soliwas etc.'[141]

~ It is highly likely that Fryderyk took to Poturzyn the first edition, dedicated to his friend, of his Variations in B flat major, written on a theme from Mozart's *Don Giovanni*, namely *La ci darem la mano, Varié pour le Piano-forte avec accompagnement d'Orchestre, dedié a Mr. Titus Woyciechowski par Frederic Chopin. Oeuvre 2*.[142]

~ We owe another addition to the map of Fryderyk's travels to the musicologist Benjamin Vogel. During his searches for pianos from Chopin's day, he came across the following inscription: 'Here also stood the brown Pleyel grand piano on which Fryderyk Chopin played on two visits to Stara Wieś from Poturzyn with his friend Tytus Woyciechowski'.[143] In his article, Vogel states that 'it was probably that piano which was the reason for those two visits to Stara Wieś'.[144]

~ Little remains from the times when Chopin stayed in Poturzyn. Tytus Woyciechowski's splendid manor house burned down, together with the sugar factory that he built, in the 1940s. Only the landscape has not undergone any fundamental changes; stretching all around are the same extensive fields on which beet is grown to this very day. There is also the park with its lakes, which at that time was certainly more impressive; today it is neglected, wild, overgrown, devoid of the necessary management of man. The remains of the farm buildings have survived, and of the sugar factory only the remnants of the foundations and parts of a red brick wall.

~ Near the old school, in the park, beneath a willow, stands a bas-relief by J. Bulewicz bearing the following inscription: 'In memory of Fryderyk Chopin, who stayed in Poturzyn at the home of his friend Tytus Woyciechowski in 1830, taking the local folk songs in his heart when, soon after, he left the country for ever'. Below this is the inscription: 'PKZ Zamość 1985'.

Poturzyn lies in the commune of Telatyn, in Tomaszów county, in the Lublin voivodeship, on the DW852, between Telatyn and Dołhobyczów.

Worth seeing in the area:
▸ Woyciechowski family tomb in Oszczów, in Hrubieszów county, about 10 km from Poturzyn,
▸ baroque timber church with two-tower facade in Tomaszów Lubelski.

Conclusion

T HE PLACES VISITED BY FRYDERYK CHOPIN on Polish soil have not previously been brought together in the form of the fullest, most reliable, compendium possible, even though they constitute an important subject and indirectly made their mark on the creative work of the most brilliant Polish composer in history.

~ The map of Chopin's journeys seems interesting for at least several reasons: it gives us some idea of the remarkable variety of the composer's experiences, be it only in relation to the people and milieux with which he became acquainted; it makes us aware of the richness of his contacts with the heterogeneous culture of Polish lands; it encompasses some of the most important Polish monuments and historical sites, from the Baltic to Wawel Hill.

~ The panorama of these places contained in this guidebook gives only an approximate picture of the impressions which the twenty-year-old composer took with him on leaving the country. Today, on the eve of the bicentenary of Chopin's birth (2010), it is easy to state how distant is the spirit of the Romantic era and how much has changed since those times. The composer's correspondence, often quoted in our guidebook, undoubtedly draws us into the atmosphere of those times and allows us to see, to a certain extent, the realities of that period through Chopin's eyes.

~ A most crucial problem, meriting a separate study, would appear to be the influence of the traditional musical culture of particular regions on Chopin's work. This question, although closely linked to the main subject of the present publication, has been barely signalled here. Research needs to be extended to include the investigation of sources and archival research in Poland, which may bring to light valuable new information and confirm or contradict many well-worn views.

~ The entirety of the experiences and impressions that Chopin gathered during his travels around Polish lands shaped the way in which he thought of his country —of his Home. In exile, these experiences underwent a gradual idealisation and sublimation, inspiring him to confide prophetically less than a year before his death: '*Terrible* things will come to pass, but at the end of it all Poland is splendid, grand, in a word: Poland.'[145]

NOTES

[1] Over the period 1772–1795, Poland was divided up over three stages by Russia, Prussia and Austria, not regaining her independence until 1918 (trans.).

[2] See P. Mysłakowski and A. Sikorski. For more detailed information, see Krzysztof Dorcz, 'Tam, gdzie urodziła się matka Chopina', 30–31.

[3] 'Patsajze tam za gulami, za gulami, jak to wilk tańcuje! A wsakzeć on nie ma zony, bo się tak frasuje (bis)' [Look o' er the mountains, o' er the mountains, how the wolf dances! And he frets so because he's not got a wife (repeat)], after *Korespondencja Fryderyka Chopina*, ed. B. E. Sydow (hereafter *KCh*), i, 45.

[4] This is discussed by Aleksander Pawlak, a scholar specialising in the music of this region, in *Folklor muzyczny Kujaw* (Cracow, 1981), 12.

[5] *KCh*, i, 68.

[6] Ibid. ii, 137.

[7] The conclusions and quotations contained in this paragraph are the result of source research, in particular a painstaking analysis of notarial documents relating to the Skarbek family, carried out by Marek Wojtylak. See M. Wojtylak, 'Tajemnice dworu w Żelazowej Woli', *Rocznik Mazowiecki*, xii (2000).

[8] In actual fact, the estate was purchased, rather than inherited, by both Fryderyk and Michał.

[9] These names are given in their work by P. Mysłakowski and A. Sikorski, *Chopinowie. Krąg rodzinno-towarzyski*, 159, referring to information taken from the *Księga hipoteczna dóbr Żelazowa Wola* [Mortgage book of the estate of Żelazowa Wola].

[10] Source as above. From the end of December 1859, for about six months, Jan Kanty Kobylański is entered as the estate's proprietor.

[11] The question of the 'emergency baptism' is discussed by Mysłakowski and Sikorski, *Chopinowie*, 148, who also analyse the subject at length in the article 'Okoliczności urodzin Fryderyka Chopina. Co mówią źródła', 28–34.

[12] Territorial battle of 972 won by Duke Mieszko I, ruler of the nascent land of Poland, over Margrave Hodo, ruler of Lusatia (trans.).

[13] *KCh*, i, 86

[14] *KCh*, i, 73.

[15] Mieczysław Tomaszewski, *Chopin. Człowiek, dzieło, rezonans*, 36

[16] See H. Wróblewska-Straus, M. Tomaszewski.

[17] Pawełek [dim. form of Paweł, Eng. Paul], son of Grand Duke Constantine.

[18] Moriolka, that is, Alexandrine de Moriolles, daughter of the French tutor, the Conte de Moriolles, a friend of Mikołaj Chopin's.

[19] *Kurier Polski*, 20 December 1829.

[20] *KCh*, i, 65.

[21] *Kurier Warszawski*, 8 March 1830.

[22] The lack of the Chodkiewicz name in biographical studies was raised by Marta Pielech in a paper delivered to the Fifth International Scholarly Conference organised by the Fryderyk Chopin Institute in Warsaw, in December 2005: The Sources of Chopin's Creative Style: Inspirations and Contexts.

²³ *KCh*, i, 110.
²⁴ Brühl Palace, also known as Ossoliński/Sandomierski Palace, stood on ul. Wierzbowa (plot no. 612) by the Saxon Garden. The palace originally belonged to the Voivode of Sandomierz, Jerzy Ossoliński. Towards the end of the seventeenth century, it was rebuilt to a design by Tylman van Gameren. It subsequently came into the possession of the Saxon minister Henryk Brühl, who initiated further rebuilding. The palace was given a late baroque appearance, with the exception of a classicist façade on the side of the splendid garden. Up to the second half of the eighteenth century, the building remained in the possession of the Brühl family. In 1787 it was purchased by the State Treasury and rebuilt to a design by Domenico Merlini; it was then that the palace gained its ballroom. At this time it housed the Russian embassy, and from 1809 the French embassy. After 1815 the palace became the residence of Grand Duke Constantine.
²⁵ This question is addressed and analysed in detail by H. F. Nowaczyk in his article 'Czy Chopin grał w pałacu Kossowskich?', 32.
²⁶ *KCh*, i, 117.
²⁷ The history of the building at 15 ul. Krakowskie Przedmieście dates back to the beginning of the eighteenth century, when it was the mansion of E. Denhoff. Soon afterwards, the building came into the possession of the Czartoryski family, and in the mid eighteenth century it was rebuilt, gaining two side wings, the 'corps-de-garde' pavilion, and also two new gates. This late baroque building was adorned with rococo sculptures by S. Ziesel. From 1782, to a commission from Izabela Lubomirska, née Czartoryska, the central portico was added and the interiors were given classicist decor. At the end of the eighteenth century, the building became the property of Stanisław Kostka Potocki and his wife, Aleksandra Potocka. At this time, Potocki Palace was one of the most magnificent magnatial seats in Warsaw. Towards the end of the nineteenth century, a new pavilion was built in the palace courtyard as an exhibition hall. It was in this pavilion that Jan Matejko's most famous works, *Hołd Pruski* [The Prussian tribute] and *Grunwald* were placed on public display for the first time in Warsaw in an art exhibition. In 1897 W. Marconi oversaw a thorough renovation of the building, which now houses the Ministry of Culture and National Heritage.
²⁸ *KCh*, i, 117.
²⁹ Inside the Church of the Holy Cross are numerous epitaphs and commemorative plaques of great Poles, including the urn with the heart of Fryderyk Chopin, which—in accordance with the composer's wishes—was brought to Poland by his elder sister, Ludwika.
³⁰ *KCh*, i, 60.
³¹ Ibid. 108.
³² K. Kobylańska (ed.), *Korespondencja Fryderyka Chopina z rodziną*, 44.
³³ T. S. Jaroszewski and M. Gierlach, *Po pałacach i dworach Mazowsza. Przewodnik. Część III*, 44.
³⁴ Aleksander Pruszak inherited from his paternal uncle the above-mentioned estates of Sanniki and Żychlin as well as a property (a palace, mansion and tenement house) on ul. Marszałkowska (plot no. 1372) in Warsaw (Pruszak House), in which Fryderyk doubtless was received many times.
³⁵ See Mysłakowski and Sikorski, *Chopinowie*, 74.

[36] See H. F. Nowaczyk.

[37] *KCh*, i, 133.

[38] The summers of the years 1820–23 were probably spent by Chopin in the countryside. These were mostly short family visits to Żelazowa Wola. Also during this period he was invited to Książenice by Mr and Mrs Marylski, the parents of his elder friend, Eustachy Marylski (1804–71), but this stay was not documented, and many older biographical studies suggest Pęcice, even though Eustachy Marylski did not acquire this estate until *c.*1830.

[39] 'For morals and diligence'—the dedication embossed on the cover of the Gaspard Monge book *Wykład statyki dla użycia szkół wydziałowych i wojewódzkich...*, trans. O. Lewocki (Warsaw, 1820) [Fr. Orig. *Traité élémentaire de la statique* (1786)]; this souvenir is held at the Fryderyk Chopin Museum in Warsaw, inv. no. M/381.

[40] For Chopin's parents, the choice of the Dziewanowskis' estate of Szafarnia as the holiday destination for their son may have had another motive besides Fryderyk's good, friendly relations with Domuś. An interesting hypothesis on this subject was put forward on the basis of their research by Piotr Mysłakowski and Andrzej Sikorski. The authors claim that the composer's father, Mikołaj Chopin, may have struck up close contacts with families from Dobrinland, and in particular with the Dziewanowskis of Szafarnia, some thirty years previously, when he was employed as a tutor. It cannot be ruled out, therefore, that Mikołaj knew most of the people and places mentioned by his son in his Szafarnia correspondence (see Mysłakowski and Sikorski, *Chopinowie*, 69–70).

[41] Sources give alternately the forenames Juliusz and Julian Ignacy Alojzy Dziewanowski.

[42] Cit. after the facsimile version of the *Kuryer* reproduced in Z. Helman (ed.), *Kurier szafarski. Faksymilia czterech autografów ze zbiorów Muzeum Chopina w Towarzystwie im. Fryderyka Chopina w Warszawie.*

[43] The Dziewanowskis of the Jastrzębiec (Bolesta) coat-of-arms, of the line of Klemens Dziewanowski of Dziewanowo, near Płock; Mysłakowski and Sikorski, *Chopinowie*, 69.

[44] Juliusz Dziewanowski was also proprietor of Bocheniec—a village named by Fryderyk in the *Kuryer Szafarski*.

[45] *KCh*, ii, 70–71.

[46] Kobylańska, *Korespondencja Fryderyka Chopina z rodziną*, 36.

[47] See K. Chruściński (ed.), *Chopin w Szafarni i okolicach*. However, this information has not been confirmed by sources.

[48] P. Dzianisz, *Okolica Chopina*, 23.

[49] *KCh*, i, 49.

[50] Ibid. 47.

[51] Ibid. 55.

[52] In Z. Jeżewska's book *Chopin w kraju rodzinnym* the name Gajewski is erroneously given as that of the then owners of Turzno. P. Dzianisz, meanwhile, in *Okolica Chopina*, gives the names Piwnicki or Szumiński. These errors also occur in other studies in which mention is made of the composer's stay in Culmland.

[53] Fryderyk visited Turzno thanks to Ksawery Zboiński, who was visiting his cousin in his native region.

[54] M. Pawłowski, *Turzno. Dzieje wsi i zespołu pałacowo-parkowego*, 40.

[55] Kobylańska, *Koryspondencja Fryderyka Chopina z rodziną*, 44.

[55] T. Zakrzewski considered these words to be exceptionally valuable, as 'essentially the earliest Polish description of our city during the times of the Prussian partition'.

[57] An estate in eastern Poland owned at the time by the Czartoryskis (trans.).

[58] *KCh*, i, 51–52.

[59] Copernicus' birthplace is now held to be the gothic tenement house at 15 ul. Kopernika.

[60] *KCh*, i, 52.

[61] Ibid.

[62] Dating of the letter by H. Wróblewska-Straus.

[63] (Franciszek-)Ksawery Zboiński was a senator and castellan of the Grand Duchy of Warsaw and senator and voivode of the Kingdom of Poland. It is worth mentioning that he purchased from Kacper Skarbek the estate of Izbica, in the Cuiavia region, on which Fryderyk Chopin's grandparents, the Krzyżanowskis, lived for several decades (see Mysłakowski and Sikorski, *Chopinowie*).

[64] During the times of Ignacy Antoni Zboiński—Castellan of Płock, husband of Salomea, née Karśnicka.

[65] M. Zduniak, 'Fryderyk Chopin we Wrocławiu i popularyzacja jego dzieł w dziewiętnastowiecznej stolicy Dolnego Śląska', 17–27.

[66] *KCh*, i, 148.

[67] Ibid.

[68] A military-civilian parish, now at 1 ul. Św. Elżbieta.

[69] See M. Zduniak, *Muzyka i muzycy polscy w dziewiętnastowiecznym Wrocławiu*, 93–99. The author also writes that 'the venue hitherto given for Chopin's performance in Wrocław, namely the hall on Plac Teatralny [...] is erroneous', 95.

[70] *KCh*, i, 69.

[71] Ibid.

[72] Ibid.

[73] Ibid.

[74] See A. Clavier, H. F. Nowaczyk.

[75] *KCh*, i, 72.

[76] See M. Zduniak.

[77] Wiktor Magnus (1833–1912) was a prominent Warsaw entrepreneur (among other things, the originator and co-founder of the Wilanów collection), music lover and relative of Fryderyk Chopin (his son, Stanisław, married the granddaughter of Dionizy Czachowski, who was Chopin's cousin three-times removed). See Mysłakowski and Sikorski, *Chopinowie*, table 5.

[78] 'To the eternal memory of Fryderyk Chopin, who in Duszniki in the year 1826 with his true art and high culture showed a noble character of spirit in his early youth, this monument, with the permission of the municipal authorities, was erected by Poles for their fellow Pole in 1897'.

[79] See P. Mysłakowski and A. Sikorski, H. F. Nowaczyk.

[80] E.g. A. Bukowski, citing sources not previously referred to in this regard, writes that Chopin accompanied on his Gdańsk expedition 'Count Zboiński of Świecie, Count Sierakowski of Waplewo and Count Dembowski with his family'.

[81] Cit. after A. Bukowski, *Pomorskie wojaże Chopina*, 30.

[82] Ibid.

[83] See P. Mysłakowski and A. Sikorski.

[84] Kobylańska, *Koryspondencja Fryderyka Chopina z rodziną*, 44.

[85] W. Kmicic-Mieleszyński, 'Sprawa pobytu Chopina w Gdańsku', 559.

[86] See A. Bukowski.

[87] See A. Bukowski.

[88] Cit. after A. Bukowski, *Waplewo. Zapomniana placówka kultury polskiej na Pomorzu Nadwiślańskim*, 109. Bukowski writes that a biography of Antoni Sierakowski was included in a work by Georg Bujack published in Koenigsberg in 1900.

[89] Ibid. 109.

[90] H. F. Nowaczyk, 'Podróż Ludwiki Chopinówny do wód Szlązkich w 1826 roku', 31.

[91] *KCh*, i, 113.

[92] A variant of this name is often given in the Chopin literature—Strzyżewo.

[93] H. F. Nowaczyk considered the work of Fryderyk's teenage sister to be an interesting biographical source: Ludwika Chopinówna, *Podróż Józia z Warszawy do wód Szlązkich przez niego samego opisana* [Little Józef's journey from Warsaw to the Silesian waters as described by himself] (Warsaw, 1830; 2nd edn, 1844).

[94] Nowaczyk writes that Chopin gave up the planned visit to Strzyżewo.

[95] Duke Antoni Radziwiłł was Prussian-appointed Governor of the Grand Duchy of Posen.

[96] *KCh*, i, 109.

[97] Chopin's visit to Antonin became a motif in the novel by Gustaw Bojanowski, *Tydzień w Antoninie*, in which the author describes in detail Chopin's stay on the Radziwiłł estate, his numerous trips to the surrounding towns and villages, walks to neighbouring villages and estates, and also a visit to Ostrów. Unfortunately, the situations described by Bojanowski, as well as the numerous names of places given as having been visited by Chopin, are for the most part unconfirmed by other sources.

[98] *KCh*, i, 112.

[99] Ibid.

[100] H. F. Nowaczyk, 'Przyczynek do dziejów eksportacji zwłok [biskupa Ignacego Krasickiego z Berlina do Gniezna: J. U. Niemcewicz, książę A. Radziwiłł, arcybiskup T. Wolicki i in.]', 9.

[101] Teofil Wolicki—a relative of the Skarbeks' (see Mysłakowski and Sikorski, *Chopinowie*).

[102] See H. F. Nowaczyk.

[103] This thread was examined in detail by H. F. Nowaczyk, who again refuted a myth that had become strongly rooted in sources.

[104] Z. Wojtkowiak, *Napisy pamiątkowe miasta Poznania*, 70.

[105] Ibid. 49.

[106] E. Goliński, *Pomniki Poznania*, 59.

[107] Archiwum Państwowe w Poznaniu, 'par. ewangelicka Żychlin, sygn. 31. Akt ślubu', see H. F. Nowaczyk, 'Kiedy Chopin „grał cudownie" na żychlińskim weselu?', 39; also Mysłakowski and Sikorski, *Chopinowie*, 106–107.

[108] 'Kronika tygodniowa', *Tygodnik Ilustrowany*, 29 Jan. 1870, 50.

[109] *KCh*, i, 106.

[110] Zofia Kossak-Szczucka, granddaughter of Aniela Gałczyńska, née Kurnatowska, referring to her grandmother's recollections, described a recital supposedly given by Chopin for the wedding guests in Żychlin in the following words: 'He was not yet famous, but he played wonderfully. It was so quiet in the hall you could hear a pin drop [...] he wasn't of good cheer and played so sadly that tears came to the eyes.' In *Dzie-dzictwo*, ii (Warsaw, 1964), 57 (cit. after Nowaczyk, 'Kiedy Chopin', 39).

[111] K. Gorczyca, *Żychlin pod Koninem. Dzieje wsi i zboru*, 81.

[112] M. Karasowski, 'Młodość Fryderyka Chopina' [Chopin's youth], *Biblioteka Warszawska*, 1862/10.

[113] The legend has it that Chopin not only passed through this village on the Oder, but even gave a recital there while waiting for a fresh team of horses. The post office and stable stood at 17/19 ul. Okrężna (building no longer extant). The postmaster invited his illustrious guests to dinner and then led them to a room with a piano, at which Chopin immediately sat down and played for two-three hours, captivating with his talent the numerous passers-by who gathered beneath the window and listened to the maestro in rapture; see L. Okowiński, *Siedem wieków Sulechowa*, 227–229.

[114] Reference to the legendary ruler of Polish prehistory, Piast the Wheelwright (trans.).

[115] Cit. from a letter to Tytus Woyciechowski in Poturzyn, *KCh*, i, 103.

[116] Cit. from a copy of the document, the last page of the school report, held at the Fryderyk Chopin Museum in Warsaw, inv. no. A/6 1973.

[117] R. Hube, introduction in *Pisma Romualda Hubego poprzedzone zarysem biograficzno-krytycznym przez Karola Dunina*, i, XXII–XXIII.

[118] K. Hoffmanowa z Tańskich, 'Przejażdżka w Krakowskie (w r. 1827)', 234.

[119] Ibid. 238.

[120] Among these exceptional buildings are also the Carolinum in Prague and the Sorbonne in Paris.

[121] Hoffmanowa z Tańskich, 'Przejażdżka', 238.

[122] Ibid. 243.

[123] Ibid. 244.

[124] Ibid. 245.

[125] Ibid. 248.

[126] Ibid. 249–250.

[127] Tomaszewski, *Chopin. Człowiek*, 37.

[128] Karasowski, *Młodość Fryderyka Chopina*, 19.

[129] In institutions such as the Jagiellonian University Museum, the Jagiellonian Library, the National Museum in Cracow and the Czartoryski Foundation attached to the National Museum in Cracow.

[130] A detailed list of Chopin souvenirs preserved in Cracow was included in L. Bularz-Różycka and B. Lewińska, *Krakowskie Chopiniana. Wystawa w 150. rocznicę śmierci Fryderyka Chopina*.

[131] Hoffmanowa, née Tańska, 'Przejażdżka', 265.

[132] Ibid. 267.

[133] Karasowski, *Młodość*, 19–20.

[134] Hoffmanowa z Tańskich, 150.

[135] Named after King Ladislaus the Elbow-high [Władysław Łokietek] (trans.).

[136] 'Chopin did indeed wish to see close-up places connected with themes from stage works produced in Warsaw: Elsner's opera *Król Łokietek* and Kurpiński's ballet *Wesele w Ojcowie*.' Cit. after T. A. Zieliński, *Chopin: życie i droga twórcza*, 108.

[137] Hoffmanowa z Tańskich, 143.

[138] Ibid. 148–149.

[139] *KCh*, i, 129.

[140] See T. Frączyk, *Warszawa młodości Chopina*, Z. Jeżewska, *Chopin w kraju rozdzinnym*.

[141] *KCh*, i, 114.

[142] H. F. Nowaczyk, 'Do Poturzyna z Wariacjami B-dur', 16.

[143] R. Aftanazy, *Dzieje rezydencji na dawnych kresach Rzeczypospolitej*, vi: *Województwo bełskie. Ziemia Chełmska województwa ruskiego*, 2nd edn (Wrocław, 1995), 178ff; see also R. Aftanazy, *Materiały do dziejów rezydencji* [Material for a history of residences], vi A (Warsaw, 1989), 234–236.

[144] B. Vogel, 'The Young Chopin's Domestic Pianos'.

[145] *KCh*, ii, 239.

Duszniki Zdrój

Sanniki

Poznań

Antonin

Oleśnica

Wrocław

Sochaczew

Szafarnia

Żelazowa Wola

Pro memoria

Chopin monuments, statues and commemorative plaques in Poland.

(Selection)

Antonin **Bust** by Marian Owczarski in the park in front of the Radziwiłł dukes' hunting palace.
Plaque at the entrance to the palace: 'Fryderyk Chopin 1810–1849 was a guest at the palace in Antonin in the years 1827 and 1829'. Founded by Igo Moś of Ostrzeszów.

Brochów **Plaque** in the Church of St John the Baptist, unveiled in 1993: 'Baptised in this church on 23 April 1810 was Fryderyk Chopin, born on 22 February 1810 at Żelazowa Wola'.

Brodnica **Bust** in the park behind the building which houses the Registry Office.

Chodaków **Bust** (iron cast on marble base) on the square in front of the Fr. Chopin Primary School

Duszniki Zdrój Obelisk in the Spa Park, unveiled on 19 June 1897, with medallion (with the composer's effigy), made from bronze. The work of Stanisław Roman Lewandowski. Beneath this, a **plaque** with a Latin inscription: 'To the eternal memory of Fryderyk Chopin, who in Duszniki in the year 1826 with his true art and high culture showed a noble character of spirit in his early youth, this monument, with the permission of the municipal authorities, was erected by Poles for their fellow Pole in 1897'.
Monument in the Spa Park, unveiled on 8 August 1976; the work of Jan Kucz.

Kozłowo **Plaque** set on a stone by the road: 'In commemoration of Fryderyk Chopin's sojourn in Kozłowo and Świecie in the summer of 1825. PTTK Świecie Branch 1985'.

Milanówek **Plaque** set into the front wall of the presbytery attached to the church of St Jadwiga, in 1986: 'At this presbytery an urn containing the heart of Fryderyk Chopin was kept from 9. IX. 1944 to 17. X. 1945'.

Bust in front of the presbytery, erected in 1998; on its base a **plaque**: 'In commemoration of the stay of the urn containing the heart of Fryderyk Chopin in the parish of St Jadwiga in Milanówek in the years 1944–1945, founded through the efforts of the Milanówek Cultural Society and the donation of Joanna and Andrzej Nowak of Milanówek. June 1998.'

Obory
Plaque in the church of the Discalced Carmelites: 'In Obory church in the summer of 1824 Fryderyk F. Chopin spent some time and played on the organ. After 175 years, in Chopin Year, 1999, Professor Mirosław Krajewski.'

Obrowo
Plaque set into the wall of the manor house on 6 August 2004: 'In this manor house, in 1824 and 1825, Fryderyk Chopin stayed and performed, also taking part in the local harvest festival, or "okrężne"'.

Oleśnica
Bust on a base (with the signature: 'Fr. Chopin') on the square in front of the historical building housing the Fr. Chopin Primary School of Music and the Lower Silesia Music Society (between ul. Kościelna and ul. Matejki).

Poturzyn
Bas-relief by J. Bulewicz: 'In memory of Fryderyk Chopin, who stayed in Poturzyn at the home of his friend Tytus Woyciechowski in 1830, taking the local folk songs in his heart when, soon after, he left the country for ever'. Below this the inscription: 'PKZ Zamość 1985'.

Poznań
Plaque with a likeness of Chopin, after a medallion by J. F. A. Bovy: 'To Chopin, 1810–1910'.
Plaque on the front wall of Poznań Municipal Offices (17 Plac Kolegiacki), unveiled on 16 October 1960: 'In 1828 Fryderyk Chopin played in this building'.
Bust in Fryderyk Chopin Park at the back of the former Jesuit college (now Poznań Municipal Offices), placed there in 1961; the work of Marcin Rożek.

Sanniki
Plaque on the front wall of the palace: 'Fryderyk Chopin stayed in this manor house in 1828'; set into the palace wall in 1925 by the then owners, Antonina Maria Dziewulska, née Natanson, and Stefan Dziewulski.

Statue in bronze in the park to the left in front of the palace; the work of Ludwika Kraskowska-Nitschowa, placed on a marble base, unveiled in 1985.

Sochaczew   **Obelisk** with a bust of the composer, unveiled in 1961 in the park on ul. Warszawska and ul. Romualda Traugutta, with the inscription 'Fryderyk Chopin 1810–1849'.

Szafarnia   **Plaque**, unveiled on 7 September 1952: 'In Szafarnia and the surrounding villages Fryderyk Chopin stayed in the years 1824–1825. In the eighth year of the existence of the People's Poland, the School in Szafarnia was named after him. 1952.'
Bust in bronze, made under the initiative of Elżbieta Buler, unveiled on 13 May 2001.

Toruń   **Plaque** at 14 ul. Mostowa: 'In this house Fryderyk Chopin stayed in the year 1825'.

Warsaw   **Monument** in the Royal Baths Park [Łazienki Królewskie] (Aleje Ujazdowskie), made by Wacław Szymanowski, unveiled in 1926, blown up by the Nazis in 1940, hence the inscription on its base: 'Statue of Fryderyk Chopin, destroyed and plundered by the Germans on 31 May 1940, rebuilt by the Nation. 17 October 1946.' After the war, the monument was reconstructed and, in 1958, restored to its original place.
Plaque with the urn containing the composer's heart in the Church of the Holy Cross, set into the second pillar, on the left-hand side of the nave. The plaque was founded by the Warsaw Music Society and unveiled in 1880. It bears a quotation from the Gospel according to St Matthew (VI.21): 'For where your treasure is, there will your heart be also'. Above this is a small bust of Chopin by Leonard Marconi.
Bas-relief after a medallion by J. F. A. Bovy at the level of the first floor of the left annexe of Casimir Palace and **plaque** commemorating the composer's residence: 'In this building lived Fryderyk Chopin in the years 1817–1827'.
Bust by Zofia Wolska by the main entrance to the departures' hall of the Fryderyk Chopin International Airport at Okęcie.
Bust in the hall opposite the main entrance to the Fryderyk Chopin Academy of Music (2 ul. Okólnik).

Plaque in the church of the Visitandine nuns set above the church door near the entrance to the chancel, founded in 1990 by the Fryderyk Chopin Society: 'In honour of Fryderyk Chopin, who played on the organ in this church as a pupil of the Warsaw Lyceum in the years 1825–1826'.

Plaque set into the front wall of the left wing of Czapski/Krasiński Palace, on the ul. Krakowskie Przedmieście side, in 1930: 'In this house Fryderyk Chopin lived and worked before leaving Warsaw for good in 1830'.

Plaque set into the front wall of the then Primary School no. 306 (at 56 ul. Połczyńska), on 2 November 1999. The plaque was founded by the Society for the Friends of Warsaw, Bemowo District Offices and Antoni Lewandowski. It commemorates the composer's departure from the capital: 'Here, on 2 November 1830, Fryderyk Chopin bade farewell to his friends, leaving his home and Poland forever'.

Plaque set into the façade of the building at 19 ul. Krakowskie Przedmieście, in memory of Wojciech Żywny, Chopin's first teacher: 'Here stood the house in which, from 1837 to 1842, lived Wojciech Żywny, Fryderyk Chopin's piano teacher'.

Plaque set into the wall of the Dziekanka building, at 56 ul. Krakowskie Przedmieście, in honour of Józef Elsner: 'Józef Elsner 1769–1854, founder of the Warsaw Conservatory, teacher of Chopin, composer and music activist, lived and worked in this house'.

Plaque near the main entrance to Zamoyski Palace, at 67/69 ul. Nowy Świat, in honour of the poet Cyprian Kamil Norwid: 'On 19 September 1863 from this building, known as Zamoyski Palace, an attack was made on the Tsar's governor Count Fyodor Berg. In retaliation, the Russian army arrested the inhabitants of the house and their possessions were thrown onto the pavement and burned. Among the items destroyed were souvenirs of Fryderyk Chopin gathered by his family including the piano on which he played as a pupil of the Warsaw Conservatory. This event was immortalised by Cyprian Norwid in his poem *Fortepian Szopena* [Chopin's piano]—the poet's tribute to the composer's genius.' This plaque was installed in 2001, thanks to an initiative from the Society for the Friends of Warsaw and the City Centre District Authorities.

Wrocław **Monument** in South Park [Park Południowy], unveiled on 24 June 2004. On the back is an inscription: 'This monument was built through the efforts of the Wrocław Branch of the Fryderyk Chopin Society and the Committee for the Building of a Fryderyk Chopin Monument, thanks to grants from the Ministry of Culture, Wrocław Municipal Government, Lower Silesia Voivodeship, Strzegom Region Stoneworkers Association, Dach Bud Ltd, Polska Miedź Foundation and donations from the public. Wrocław 5 IX 2005.'

Żelazowa Wola **Obelisk** in the park, unveiled in 1894, with medallion and bust of the composer, the inscription 'F. Chopin 22. II. 1810', and below this a lyre among leaves. It was designed by Bronisław Żochowski.
Bust in sandstone by Stanisław Sikora, in the park, unveiled in 1968.
Statue in bronze on a base of grey granite, in the park; the work of Józef Gosławski; unveiled in 1969.
Bust on a sandstone plinth, in the park, made by Zofia Wolska.

Żychlin **Plaque** on the front wall of the palace in Żychlin: 'Here, in the first days of September 1829, stayed Fryderyk Chopin'. Unveiled on 2 September 1999 under the initiative of Henryk Janasek.

Useful addresses

WARSAW

Fryderyk Chopin Institute [Narodowy Instytut Fryderyka Chopina]
Plac Piłsudskiego 9, 00-078 Warszawa,
tel. (+ 48 22) 826 24 75, 827 54 71, 827 54 72, 828 02 50;
http://www.chopin.nifc.pl/; email: nifc@nifc.pl, sales@nifc.pl

International Federation of Chopin Societies
[Międzynarodowa Federacja Towarzystw Chopinowskich]
Plac Piłsudskiego 9, 00-078 Warszawa (2nd floor),
tel. (+ 48 22) 826 24 75, 827 54 71, 827 54 72, 828 02 50; ext. 138, 139

Polish Chopin Academy [Polska Akademia Chopinowska]
Plac Piłsudskiego 9, 00-078 Warszawa (2nd floor),
tel. (+ 48 22) 826 24 75, 827 54 71, 827 54 72, 828 02 50; ext. 138, 139

Fryderyk Chopin Society [Towarzystwo im. Fryderyka Chopina]
Plac Piłsudskiego 9, 00-078 Warszawa,
tel. (+ 48 22) 827 95 89, 826 65 49, 828 38 73;
http://www.chopin.pl/

Foundation for the National Edition of the Works of Fryderyk Chopin
[Fundacja Wydania Narodowego Dzieł Fryderyka Chopina]
ul. Okólnik 2, pok. 405, 00-368 Warszawa,
tel. (+ 48 22) 827 72 41, ext. 256
http://www.chopin-nationaledition.com/
email: fundwn@chopin.edu.pl, fundacja@chopin-nationaledition.com

Fryderyk Chopin Museum [Muzeum Fryderyka Chopina]
Pałac Ostrogskich, ul. Okólnik 1, 00-368 Warszawa,
tel. (+ 48 22) 827 54 73, 826 59 38

Chopin Family Drawing Room [Salonik Chopinów]
Pałac Czapskich-Krasińskich, Akademia Sztuk Pięknych,
Krakowskie Przedmieście 5, 00-068 Warszawa,
tel. (+ 48 22) 826 62 51, ext. 267

ANTONIN
Radziwiłł Dukes' Hunting Palace, Centre for Creative Work
[Pałac Myśliwski Książąt Radziwiłłów, Dom Pracy Twórczej]
63-422 Antonin, tel./fax (+ 48 62) 736 16 51, tel. (+ 48 62) 734 81 14, 734 81 69

DUSZNIKI ZDRÓJ
Foundation for the International Chopin Festival
[Fundacja Międzynarodowych Festiwali Chopinowskich]
Rynek 10, 57-340 Duszniki Zdrój,
tel./fax (+ 48 74) 866 92 80, http://www.chopin.festival.pl/; email: chopin@festival.pl

SANNIKI
Sanniki Palace [Pałac w Sannikach]
ul. Warszawska 142, 09-540 Sanniki,
tel. (+ 48 24) 277 60 58, 277 61 70,
http://www.palacsanniki.pl/; email: palac.sanniki@op.pl

SZAFARNIA
Szafarnia Chopin Centre [Ośrodek Chopinowski w Szafarnia]
87-404 Radomin, tel./fax (+ 48 56) 682 79 30,
http://www.szafarnia.art.pl/

ŻELAZOWA WOLA
Birthplace of Fryderyk Chopin, Żelazowa Wola
[Dom Urodzenia Fryderyka Chopina Żelazowa Wola]
Żelazowa Wola, 96-503 Sochaczew,
tel. (+ 48 46) 863 33 00; fax (+ 48 46) 863 40 76

BIBLIOGRAPHY

Antkowiak, Z., *Kościoły Wrocławia* [The churches of Wrocław] (Wrocław, 1991).

Błaszczak, K., and Makuliński, M., *Chopin na Mazowszu. Mazowiecki program obchodów 150. rocznicy śmierci Fryderyka Chopina. Informator* [Chopin in Mazovia. The Mazovia programme for the commemoration of the 150th anniversary of the death of Fryderyk Chopin. An informational guide] (Warsaw, 1999).

Bujak, A., *Zamki i warownie w Polsce* [Castles and strongholds in Poland], comm. Anna Szczucka (Warsaw, 1998).

—*Katedry Polskie* [Polish cathedrals], intr. Stanisław Bogdanowicz, historical notes Tomasz Jaworski (Cracow, 1997).

—*Wawel. Katedra i zamek* [Wawel Hill. The cathedral and castle], text Jan K. Ostrowski (Cracow, 2004).

Bukowski, A., *Pomorskie wojaże Chopina* [Chopin's travels in Pomerania] (Gdańsk, 1993).

—*Waplewo. Zapomniana placówka kultury polskiej na Pomorzu Nadwiślańskim* [Waplewo. A forgotten post of Polish culture in Eastern Pomerania] (Wrocław, 1989).

Bularz-Różycka, L., and Lewińska, B., *Krakowskie Chopiniana. Wystawa w 150. rocznicę śmierci Fryderyka Chopina* [Cracow Chopiniana. An exhibition on the 150th anniversary of the death of Fryderyk Chopin] (Cracow, 1999).

Chlebowski, B., Sulimirski, F., and Walewski, W. (eds.), *Słownik geograficzny Królestwa Polskiego i innych krajów słowiańskich* [A geographical dictionary of the Kingdom of Poland and other Slavic lands], 15 vols. (Warsaw, 1880–1902).

Chotomska, W., *Tam, gdzie był Chopin* [Where Chopin set foot] (Warsaw, 1990).

Chruściński, K. (ed.), *«Szafarnia moje uszanowanie». Chopin na ziemi dobrzyńskiej* ['Szafarnia, my respects'. Fryderyk Chopin in Dobrinland] (Szafarnia and Rypin, 2004).

—(ed.), *Chopin w Szafarni i okolicach. Vademecum turystyczne* [Chopin in Szafarnia and the surrounding area. A guide] (Golub-Dobrzyń, 1995).

Clavier, A., *Dans l'entourage de Chopin* (Lens, 1984).

Czerniewicz-Umer, T., and Omilanowska, M. (eds.), *Polska* [Poland] (Warsaw, 2002).

Czerwińska, T., *Zabytki i Muzea Chopinowskie w Polsce. Przewodnik turystyczny* [Chopin monuments and museums in Poland. A touristic guide] (Warsaw, 1986).

Czyńska, Z., et al., *Cmentarz Powązkowski w Warszawie* [Powązki Cemetery in Warsaw] (Warsaw, 1984).

Dorcz, K., 'Tam, gdzie urodziła się matka Chopina' [Where Chopin's mother was born], *Ruch Muzyczny*, 2000/15, 30–31.

Drexlerowa, A. M. (ed.), *Kultura Miejska w Królestwie Polskim. Cz. I, 1815–1875* [Urban culture in the Kingdom of Poland. Part I: 1815–1875] (Warsaw, 2001).

Dzianisz, P., *Okolice Chopina* [Around Chopin] (Gdynia, 1964).

—*Kuryer Szafarski, Wakacyjna gazeta Fryderyka Chopina z sierpnia – września 1824 r.* [The Szafarnia Courier. Fryderyk Chopin's holiday gazette from August-September 1824] (Pelplin, 1999).

Eberhardt, P., *Polska i jej granice. Z historii polskiej geografii politycznej* [Poland and her borders. On the history of Polish political geography] (Lublin, 2004).

Estreicher, K., *Muzeum Uniwersytetu Jagiellońskiego* [Jagiellonian University Museum] (Warsaw and Cracow, 1980).

Frączyk, T., *Warszawa młodości Chopina* [The Warsaw of Chopin's youth] (Cracow, 1961).

Goliński, E., *Pomniki Poznania* [The monuments of Poznań] (Poznań, 2001).

Gołąb, M., 'Studia Fryderyka Chopina w Szkole Głównej Muzyki Królewskiego Uniwersytetu Warszawskiego' [Fryderyk Chopin's studies at the High School of Music of the Royal University of Warsaw], in J. Miziołek (ed.), *Kultura artystyczna Uniwersytetu Warszawskiego* [The artistic culture of Warsaw University] (Warsaw, 2003), 59–69.

Gorczyca, K., *Żychlin pod Koninem. Dzieje wsi i zboru* [Żychlin near Konin. History of the village and parish] (Warsaw, 1997).

Grudziński, A. A., *Kult Chopina w Polsce* [The cult of Chopin in Poland] (Poznań, 1995).

Helbich, A., 'Kronika tygodniowa' [Weekly chronicle], *Tygodnik ilustrowany*, 1870/109, 50.

Helman, Z. (ed.), *Kurier szafarski. Faksymilia czterech autografów ze zbiorów Muzeum Chopina w Towarzystwie im. Fryderyka Chopina w Warszawie* [Szafarnia Courier. Facsimiles of four autographs from the Chopin Museum Collection at the Fryderyk Chopin Society in Warsaw] (Gdańsk and Warsaw, 1999).

Herz, L., *Mazowsze* [Mazovia] (Warsaw, 2000).

Hoesick., F., *Chopin. Życie i twórczość. Tom I, Warszawa 1810–1831* [Chopin. His life and work. Vol. I: Warsaw 1810–1831] (Warsaw, 1967).

Hoffmanowa z Tańskich, K., 'Przejażdżka w Krakowskie (w r. 1827)' [A journey to the region of Cracow (in 1827)], in *Rozrywki dla dzieci* [Amusement for children], iv: *Opisy niektórych okolic Polski / przez Autorkę pamiątki po dobrej matce* [Descriptions of certain parts of Poland / to the memory of a good mother] (Warsaw: S. H. Merzbach, 1859), 103–316.

Hordyński, W., 'Pamiątki po Chopinie w zbiorach krakowskich' [Chopin souvenirs in Cracow collections], *Kwartalnik Muzyczny*, 1949/26–27, 378–389.

—'Chopin w Bibliotece Jagiellońskiej' [Chopin in the Jagiellonian Library], *Ruch Muzyczny*, 1959/14, 2–3.

Hube, R., *Romualda Hubego Pisma* [The writings of Romuald Hube], intr. Karol Dunin, i (Warsaw, 1905).

Ihnatowicz, I., *Nauki pomocnicze historii XIX i XX wieku* [Complementary studies for the history of the 19th and 20th c.] (Warsaw, 1990).

Iwaszkiewicz, J., *Chopin* (Cracow, 1984).

Jaroszewski, T. S., and Baraniewski, W., *Po pałacach i dworach Mazowsza. Przewodnik* [A guide to the palaces and manors of Mazovia], i (2nd edn, Warsaw, 1999).

—and Gierlach, M., *Po pałacach i dworach Mazowsza. Przewodnik* [A guide to the palaces and manors of Mazovia], iii (Warsaw, 1998).

Jeżewska, Z., *Chopin w kraju rodzinnym* [Chopin in his native land] (Warsaw, 1985).

Kajzer, L., *Leksykon zamków w Polsce* [A lexicon of castles in Poland] (Warsaw, 2001).

Karasowski, M., 'Młodość Fryderyka Chopina' [Fryderyk Chopin's youth], *Biblioteka Warszawska*, 1862/10.

Kazimierski, J., and Kołodziejczyk, R. (eds.), *Dzieje Mazowsza i Warszawy: wybór źródeł* [The history of Mazovia and Warsaw: a selection of sources] (Warsaw, 1973).

Kmicic-Mieleszyński, W., 'Sprawa pobytu Chopina w Gdańsku' [The question of Chopin's sojourn in Gdańsk], in Z. Lissa (ed.), *The Book of the First International Congress Devoted to the Works of Frederick Chopin* (Warsaw, 1963), 559.

Kobielski, D., *Warszawa na fotografiach* [Warsaw in photographs] (Warsaw, 1982).

Kobylańska, K., *Chopin w kraju: dokumenty i pamiątki* (Cracow, 1955); Eng. trans. as *Chopin in his Own Land*, trans. C. Grece-Dąbrowska and M. Filippi (Warsaw, 1955).

—*Korespondencja Fryderyka Chopina z rodziną* [Fryderyk Chopin's correspondence with his family] (Warsaw, 1972).

Kopeć, J., and Skowroński, J., *Śladami Fryderyka Chopina. Polska. Europa* [In the footsteps of Fryderyk Chopin. Poland. Europe] (Warsaw, 2000).

Korespondencja Fryderyka Chopina [The correspondence of Fryderyk Chopin], ed. B. E. Sydow, 2 vols. (Warsaw, 1955).

Krasiński, J. W., *Przewodnik dla Podhorążych w Polsce i Rzeczpospolitej Krakowskiej* [Guide for cadets in Poland and the Republic of Cracow] (Warsaw, 1821).

Michałowski, K., *Bibliografia Chopinowska 1849–1969* [Chopin bibliography 1849–1969] (Cracow, 1970 (supplements in *Rocznik Chopinowski*, 9 (1975), 11 (1979), 12 (1980) and 13 (1981)).

Mirska, M., *Szlakiem Chopina* [On Chopin's trail] (Warsaw, 1949).

Miziołek, J. (ed.), *Kultura artystyczna Uniwersytetu Warszawskiego* [The artistic culture of Warsaw University] (Warsaw, 2003).

Mysłakowski, P., *Rodzina ojca Chopina. Migracja i awans* [The family of Chopin's father. Migration and social advancement] (Warsaw, 2002).

—and Sikorski, A., *Chopinowie. Krąg rodzinno-towarzyski* [The Chopins. Their family and social circle] (Warsaw, 2005).

— —'Okoliczności przyjazdu Mikołaja Chopina do Polski' [The circumstances surrounding Mikołaj Chopin's arrival in Poland], *Ruch Muzyczny*, 2004/18, 33–38.

— —'Okoliczności urodzin Fryderyka Chopina. Co mówią źródła' [The circumstances surrounding the birth of Fryderyk Chopin. What the sources say], *Ruch Muzyczny*, 2002/20, 28–34.

— — 'Recenzja pracy [review of]: G. Ladaique, *Les origines lorraines de Frédéric Chopin*, Sarreguemines 1999', *Rocznik Polskiego Towarzystwa Heraldycznego*, new ser., 5 (Warsaw, 2002), 202–207.

— — 'Zboińscy z Kowalewa a rodzina Chopina' [The Zboińskis of Kowalewo and Chopin's family], *Ruch Muzyczny*, 2004/20, 50–54.

Nowaczyk, H. F., *Chopin na traktach Wielkopolski Południowej* [Chopin on the highways of southern Greater Poland] (Kalisz, 2006).

—'Chopin nie grał w Sulechowie' [Chopin did not play in Sulechów], *Ruch Muzyczny*, 1996/1, 31–33 and 1996/2, 33–35.

—'Chopin w pałacu arcybiskupów w Poznaniu' [Chopin at the Archbishops' Palace in Poznań], *Ruch Muzyczny*, 1997/19, 31–34.

—'Czy Chopin grał w Pałacu Kossowskich?' [Did Chopin play at Kossowski Palace?], *Ruch Muzyczny*, 1999/11, 29–33 and 1999/12, 32.

—'Czy Chopin wytchnął „u Flammów w Kaliszu"' [Did Chopin rest 'at the Flamms' in Kalisz?'], *Ruch Muzyczny*, 1999/11, 23–25 and 1999/12, 31–33.

—'Do Poturzyna z Wariacjami B-dur' [To Poturzyn with the B flat major Variations], *Ruch Muzyczny*, 1998/18, 33–35 and 1998/19, 34–35.

—'Epizod z pobytu Chopina w Poznaniu' [An episode from Chopin's stay in Poznań], *Ruch Muzyczny*, 1999/4, 32–35.

—'Jak Chopin dyliżansował do Kalisza' [How Chopin travelled by stagecoach to Kalisz], *Ruch Muzyczny*, 1995/4, 35–37.

—'Kiedy Chopin grał cudownie na żychlińskim weselu?' [When did Chopin play wonderfully at a wedding in Żychlin?], *Ruch Muzyczny*, 2000/16, 37–41.

—'Koncert Chopina w obozie 3. brygady piechoty' [Chopin's concert in the camp of the 3rd infantry brigade], *Ruch Muzyczny*, 2001/4, 32–35.

—'Koncert, którego nie było. Przypisy do inskrypcji na siedzibie prezydenta Poznania' [The concert that never was. Notes to an inscription on the mayor's palace in Poznań], *Ruch Muzyczny*, 1995/1, 9–13.

—'Lato 1826 roku w „Reinertz"' [The summer of 1826 in 'Reinertz'], *Ruch Muzyczny*, 2000/10, 28–32.

—'Na czyim weselu był Chopin w Żychlinie' [Whose wedding reception Chopin attended in Żychlin], *Ruch Muzyczny*, 1996/8, 36–39.

—'Ostatnia podróż Chopina między Wisłą a Prosną Lato 1826 roku' [Chopin's last journey between the Vistula and Prosna rivers in the summer of 1826], *Ruch Muzyczny*, 1996/10, 36–39.

—'Podróż Chopina w hrubieszowskie strony' [Chopin's journey in the direction of Hrubieszów], *Ruch Muzyczny*, 1997/4, 28–31.

—'Podróż Ludwiki Chopinówny „do wód Szlązkich" w 1826 roku' [Ludwika Chopin's journey 'to the Silesian waters' in 1826], *Ruch Muzyczny*, 2000/4, 32–35.

—'Przyczynek do dziejów eksportacji zwłok [biskupa Ignacego Krasickiego z Berlina do Gniezna: J. U. Niemcewicz, książę A. Radziwiłł, arcybiskup T. Wolicki i in.]' [On the history of the exportation of the body [of Bishop Ignacy Krasicki from Berlin to Gniezno: J. U. Niemcewicz, Duke A. Radziwiłł, Archbishop T. Wolicki et al]], *Ruch Muzyczny*, 1995/29, 9.

Nowik, W., 'Kultura muzyczna Warszawy czasów Chopina' [The musical culture of Warsaw in Chopin's times], *Rocznik Warszawski*, 30 (2002), 53–93.

—'Relacje pomiędzy Józefem Elsnerem a Fryderykiem Chopinem w świetle korespondencji' [The relations between Józef Elsner and Fryderyk Chopin in the light of correspondence], in S. Paczkowski (ed.), *Muzyka wobec tracycji. Idee – dzieło – recepcja* [Music and tradition. Ideas, the work and reception] (Warsaw, 2004), 443–453.

Okowiński, L., *Siedem wieków Sulechowa. Szkice z dziejów miasta i okolic od pradziejów do 1945 r.* [Seven centuries of Sulechów. Sketches from the history of the town and its surrounding area from prehistory to 1945] (Sulechów, 2000).

Olejniczak, M., *Strzyżew monografia wsi 1295–1995* [Strzyżew. Monograph of the village 1295–1995] (Ostrów Wielkopolski, 1995).

Omilanowska, M., and Majewski, J. S., *Warszawa* [Warsaw] (Warsaw, 2000).

Oniszczuk-Awiżeń, K. (ed.), *Zaczęło się w Bad Reinerz... Tradycje muzyczne Dusznik Zdroju* [It began in Bad Reinerz. The musical traditions of Duszniki Zdrój] (Kłodzko, 2005).

Pawłowski, M., *Gmina Obrowo. Przeszłość i teraźniejszość* [The commune of Obrowo. Past and present (Toruń, 1996).

—*Turzno. Dzieje wsi i zespołu pałacowo-parkowego* [Turzno. A history of the village and the palace-park complex] (Toruń, 1996).

Pilich, M., *Warszawa w 3 dni* [Warsaw in three days] (Warsaw, 2003).

Podlecki, J., *Wieliczka* (Cracow, 2001).

Poniatowska, I., 'Chopin – Liszt. Kontakty artystów i oddziaływania stylistyczne' [Chopin and Liszt. Artistic contacts and stylistic influence], in *Chopin w kręgu przyjaciół* [Chopin in his circle of friends], i (Warsaw, 1995).

Prinke, R., 'Recenzja pracy [review of]: A. Sikorski, P. Mysłakowski, *Rodzina matki Chopina. Mity i rzeczywistość*. Warsaw 2000', in *Rocznik Polskiego Towarzystwa Heraldycznego* [Yearbook of the Polish Heraldry Society], new ser., v (Warsaw, 2002), 207–213.

Przybylski, R., *Cień jaskółki: esej o myślach Chopina* [A swallow's shadow: an essay on Chopin's thoughts] (Cracow, 1995).

Sikorski, A., and Mysłakowski, P., *Rodzina matki Chopina. Mity i rzeczywistość* [The family of Chopin's mother. Myths and reality] (Warsaw, 2000).

Siwkowska, J., *Pan Chopin opuszcza Warszawę* [Mr Chopin leaves Warsaw] (Warsaw, 1958).

—*Tam gdzie Chopin chodził na pół czarnej. Stylizacje* [Where Chopin would go for a coffee. Stylisations] (Warsaw, 1959).

—'Życie miasta w latach 1810–1830' [Life in the city in the years 1810–1830], in *Warszawa miasto Chopina* [Warsaw: Chopin's city], collective work (Warsaw, 1950), 51–94.

Szczepański, J., *Sanniki i okolice* [Sanniki and the surrounding area] (Warsaw, 1987).

Szulc, M. A., *Fryderyk Chopina i utwory jego muzyczne* [Fryderyk Chopin and his musical works], Biblioteka Chopinowska (Warsaw, 1986).

Tomaszewska, W., 'Chopin w Dusznikach' [Chopin in Duszniki], in K. Kościukiewicz (ed.), *Międzynarodowe Festiwale Chopinowskie w Dusznikach Zdroju 1946–1999* [The International Chopin Festival in Duszniki Zdrój 1946–1999] (Wrocław, 2000), 10–16.

Tomaszewski, M., *Chopin. Człowiek, dzieło, rezonans* [Chopin. The man, his work and its resonance] (2nd edn, Cracow, 2005).

—'Chopin', in *Encyklopedia Muzyczna*, ii: *cd* (Cracow, 1984).

—and Weber, B., *Diariusz par image* [A diary in images] (Warsaw, 1990).

Vogel, B., 'The Young Chopin's Domestic Pianos', in A. Szklener (ed.), *Chopin in Performance: History, Theory, Practice* (Warsaw, 2004), 57–75.

Weber, B., *Chopin* (Wrocław, 2003).

Wojtkowiak, Z., *Napisy pamiątkowe miasta Poznania* [Commemorative inscriptions in the city of Poznań] (Poznań, 2004).

Wójcicki, K. W., *Cmentarz Powązkowski pod Warszawą* [Powązki Cemetery near Warsaw], 3 vols. (Warsaw: S. Orgelbrand, 1855–1858).

Wróblewska-Straus, H., and Markiewicz, K., *Fryderyk Chopin i bracia Kolbergowie na tle epoki. Przyjaźń, praca, fascynacje* [Fryderyk Chopin and the Kolberg brothers in the context of their era. Friendship, work and fascinations], exhibition catalogue (Warsaw, 2005).

Zakrzewski, T. (ed.), *Młody Fryderyk Chopin w Toruniu: list Fryderyka Chopina do Jana Matuszyskiego w Warszawie: Szafarnia 1825* [The young Fryderyk Chopin in Toruń. Fryderyk Chopin's letter to Jan Matuszyński in Warsaw, Szafarnia 1825] (Toruń, 1984).

Załuscy, P. and I., and Komarniccy, H. and J., *Szlakiem Chopina po Polsce* [On Chopin's trail around Poland] (Warsaw, 2000).

Zduniak, M., 'Fryderyk Chopin we Wrocławiu i popularyzacja jego dzieł w dziewiętnastowiecznej stolicy Dolnego Śląska' [Fryderyk Chopin in Wrocław and the popularisation of his works in the 19th-century capital of Lower Silesia], in K. Kościukiewicz (ed.), *Międzynarodowe Festiwale Chopinowskie w Dusznikach Zdroju 1946–1999* [The International Chopin Festival in Duszniki Zdrój 1946–1999] (Wrocław, 2000), 17–27.

—*Muzyka i muzycy polscy w dziewiętnastowiecznym Wrocławiu* [Polish music and musicians in 19th-century Wrocław] (Wrocław, 1984).

Zieliński, T. A., *Chopin: życie i droga twórcza* [Chopin. His life and creative path] (Cracow, 1993).

Żuchowski, L., Kowalski, R., and Karasiński, M. (eds.), *Powiat Golubsko-Dobrzyński* [Golub-Dobrzyń county] (Toruń, 1999).

INDEX OF NAMES

INDEX OF PLACES

ILLUSTRATIONS

Abbreviations:
AMU - Adam Mickiewicz University [Uniwersytet im. Adama Mickiewicza] in Poznań
FCI – Fryderyk Chopin Institute [Narodowy Instytut Fryderyka Chopina] in Warsaw
NL – National Library [Biblioteka Narodowa] in Warsaw
NMW – National Museum [Muzeum Narodowe] in Warsaw
WUL - Warsaw University Library [Biblioteka Uniwersytecka w Warszawie]

p. 6   Windmill, pencil drawing by Fryderyk Chopin, FCI photographic collection.

p. 14   Żelazowa Wola, Fryderyk Chopin's birthplace, drawing by Lenc, *Tygodnik Ilustrowany*, 1891/11, photo by P. Mysłakowski, photographer's own collection.

p. 16   Żelazowa Wola, with the Skarbeks' manor house, woodcut by I. Chełmicki after Bolesław Jaworski, 1870, FCI photographic collection.

p. 20   Church of St Roch in Brochów, drawing signed 'Wł. Gościmski'; FCI photographic collection, F. 7884; photo by T. Konart.

p. 21   Saxon Palace, colour lithograph by L. Schmidtner, first half of 19th c., from an album of architectural drawings, fasc. 2, table 46, NL, Dział Ikonografii T. II-7, G. 4715; photo by E. Gawryszewska.

p. 24   Saxon Garden, Mineral Water Pavilion, lithograph by F. Bruder, NL, Dział Ikonografii nr inw. Gr. Pol. 1248, neg. nr 99224; photo by H. Romanowski.

p. 26   Casimir Palace, water colour by J. F. Piwarski, *c.*1824, NLW, Rys. Pol. 4200; photo by P. Ligier.

p. 29   View of ul. Krakowskie Przedmieście around Czapski/Krasiński Palace, aquatint by K. F. Dietrich, 1830, FCI photographic collection.

p. 30   *Salon Chopinów w Pałacu Krasińskich* [The Chopins' drawing-room in Czapski/Krasiński Palace], quill sketch by A. Kolberg, 1832; L. Binental, 1930, FCI photographic collection.

p. 33   Casimir Palace, lithograph by L. Schmidtner, first half of 19th c., from an album of architectural drawings, fasc. 2, table 22, NL, Dział Ikonografii T. II-7, G. 1087.

p. 34   The monastery buildings housed the Music Conservatory. Aquatint by B. Belotto [Canaletto] after his own oil painting, 1771. FCI photographic collection.

p. 37   Map of Warsaw University campus and 'Botanika', 1817–18, in J. Miziołek (ed.), *Kultura artystyczna Uniwersytetu Warszawskiego* (Warsaw, 2002), 35.

p. 38   Home of the Warsaw Society for the Friends of Learning, lithograph by L. Schmidtner, first half of 19th c., from an album of architectural drawings, table 46, NL, Dział Ikonografii T. II-7, G. 1093; photo by E. Gawryszewska.

p. 43   Radziwiłł Palace (Governor's Palace) (in *Gabinet czytania...*), lithograph by K. F. Dietrich, first half of 19th c., NL, Dzial Ikonografii, WAF. 663, G. 34025.

p. 45   Building of the Warsaw Charitable Society, lithograph by K. Pilatti, in A. Sokołowski, *Dzieje porozbiorowe narodu polskiego ilustrowane* (Warsaw, nd), iv, 98, NMW Library, shelf-mark HP III 202; photo by P. Ligier.

p. 47   Belvedere, lithograph by K. F. Dietrich, first half of 19th c. (in *Gabinet czytania...*), NL, T-1 -33, G. 115244.

ACKNOWLEDGEMENTS

We wish to express our gratitude for inspiring us to explore and research *Chopin's Poland* to Professors Irena Poniatowska, Zofia Chechlińska, Jan Ekier, Halina Goldberg, Bohdan Pociej, Zbigniew Skowron, Piotr Dahlig, José O. Albán Ramos and the originator of the project, Grzegorz Michalski.

Our thanks go to Piotr Mysłakowski for his valuable hints and assistance in our work on the book. For their time and kindness, we also thank Krystyna Bentkowska, Elżbieta Artysz, Aleksandra Głowacka, Henryk Janasek, Mieczysław Kłos, Marek Pawłowski, Michał Kokot and Jacek Weiss.

Marita Albán Juárez and Ewa Sławińska-Dahlig

Factual consultant
Piotr Mysłakowski

Graphic design, layout and typesetting
Grzegorz Laszuk K+S

Contemporary photographs
Ewa Sławińska-Dahlig

Translated and edited by
John Comber

Cover illustration
*Fryderyk Chopin, c.*1829, after an oil portrait by Ambroży Mieroszewski

Printed and bound by
Agencja Reklamowo-Wydawnicza Arkadiusz Grzegorczyk
www.grzeg.com.pl

Maps
Dom Wydawniczy Elipsa
Małgorzata Butkiewicz, Marta Grabarczyk
www.elipsa.pl

Published by

NARODOWY
INSTYTUT
FRYDERYKA
CHOPINA

Narodowy Instytut Fryderyka Chopina
Pl. Piłsudskiego 9, 00-078 Warszawa
www.chopin.nifc.pl

ISBN: 978-83-61142-03-4

MAP OF POLAND

O place associated with Fryderyk Chopin
⋯ place where Chopin's presence
  is insufficiently documented

Not marked on the map are places which
Chopin merely passed through